Colosseum

Guide 2024-2025

A Journey through Italy's Ancient Heart, Uncovering the Secrets, Stories, and Splendors of the World's Most Iconic Amphitheater

Robert D. Richmond

1

TABLE OF CONTENTS

Scan the QR code for an exclusive map of the Colosseum and its surroundings. Let this guide be your key to unlocking the secrets of Rome's ancient marvel.

INTRODUCTION

Welcome to the Colosseum

Stepping off the cobblestone streets of Rome and gazing up at the towering structure before me, I was hit by a wave of awe that nearly astounded me. The Colosseum, with its massive, weathered arches and imposing presence, stood like a timeless guardian of history, silently telling stories of an era long past yet vividly alive in the cracks and crevices of its ancient stones. It was not just another tourist site; it was a monumental piece of the human story, and here I was, standing at its feet, feeling like I had just opened a door into a different world.

I remember the first time I truly understood what the Colosseum represented. It was not during a lecture in school or from the pages of a history book, but in the moment, I saw it with my own eyes. I had always known it as the iconic symbol of Rome, the grand arena where gladiators fought and emperors watched. Nevertheless, being there, seeing it in person changed everything. It was as if the Colosseum whispered its secrets to me, unraveling the tales of its construction, the cheers of the crowds, and the blood that had soaked its sands.

The approach to the Colosseum is almost as thrilling as the sight itself. Walking through Rome's bustling streets, there is a sense of anticipation that builds with every step. The city around you is alive with history—every corner, every stone has a story to tell. Then, as you turn a corner or crest a small hill, the Colosseum suddenly comes into view, and the rest of the world fades away. It is like a time portal; one moment you are in the heart of a modern city, and the next, you are transported back to ancient Rome.

The first thing that struck me was the sheer scale of it. Pictures don't do it justice. It is only when you are standing next to those towering walls, craning your neck to see the top that you begin to appreciate the ingenuity and ambition that went into its construction. Each archway, each pillar is a testament to the engineering marvels of the ancient Romans. It is easy to lose yourself in the details—the worn steps, the faint carvings, the vastness of the arena floor where so much history unfolded.

As I wandered through the Colosseum, I could almost hear the echoes of the past—the roar of the crowds, the clashing of swords, the tense moments before a fight began. I could imagine the sun beating down on the spectators as they watched, enraptured by the spectacle before them. The Colosseum is not just a ruin; it is a living, breathing monument to the past, filled with stories waiting to be discovered by those who walk its corridors.

Leaving the Colosseum, I felt a deep sense of connection to history. This was not just a visit to an ancient site; it was a journey into the heart of human civilization. The Colosseum is more than a destination—it is an experience, one that leaves you with a profound respect for the people who came before us and the stories they left behind. Moreover, as I walked away, I knew that this place had changed me in a way that no other destination ever could.

Historical Overview

The Colosseum, originally known as the Flavian Amphitheatre, stands as one of the most iconic symbols of ancient Rome. Its construction began under Emperor Vespasian in AD 72 and was completed in AD 80 by his son, Emperor Titus. The amphitheater was built on the site of Nero's former palace, the Domus Aurea, as a gesture to return a portion of Rome to the people after years of imperial excess. Vespasian's decision to construct the

Colosseum on this site symbolized a new era of leadership, focused on public welfare and entertainment.

The Colosseum was officially inaugurated in AD 80 with a series of games and spectacles that lasted for 100 days. These events included gladiatorial combats, animal hunts, and even mock naval battles, which showcased the engineering prowess of the Romans. The amphitheater could accommodate up to 50,000 spectators, with seating arranged according to social rank, from senators and nobility at the front to the common people in the upper tiers.

Over the next few centuries, the Colosseum remained a central venue for public entertainment, particularly gladiatorial contests, which continued until the early 5th century. However, as the Western Roman Empire began to decline, the frequency and scale of these events diminished. By the 6th century, with the spread of Christianity and changing societal values, the gladiatorial games were gradually phased out, and the Colosseum's purpose began to shift.

During the medieval period, the Colosseum underwent significant changes. It was repurposed for various uses, including housing, workshops, and even a fortress for Roman noble families. By the 12th century, it had been heavily damaged by earthquakes and the stone was pillaged for the construction of other buildings in Rome, including St. Peter's Basilica. Despite its declining structural integrity, the Colosseum remained a powerful symbol of Rome's former glory.

The Renaissance period brought renewed interest in ancient Roman architecture, and the Colosseum was partially restored. However, it wasn't until the 18th and 19th centuries that serious preservation efforts began, spurred by the increasing awareness of the importance of preserving cultural heritage. Restoration projects during this time aimed to stabilize the structure and prevent further deterioration.

Today, the Colosseum stands as a monument to Rome's architectural and cultural legacy. Although it has endured centuries of wear and tear, it continues to attract millions of visitors annually, serving as a powerful reminder of the grandeur of ancient Rome and the enduring impact of its civilization.

Importance in Roman Culture

The Colosseum, known as the Flavian Amphitheatre, was not just an architectural marvel but a cornerstone of public life and culture in ancient Rome. Its cultural significance extended far beyond its massive structure, symbolizing the might and grandeur of the Roman Empire.

Constructed between 70-80 AD, the Colosseum served as the epicenter of Roman entertainment, hosting a variety of public spectacles that were integral to the social and political fabric of the city. The games held in the Colosseum were more than mere entertainment; they were a demonstration of Rome's power, wealth, and control over nature and its conquered peoples.

One of the most significant aspects of the Colosseum was its role in the gladiatorial games. These brutal combats, often between slaves, prisoners of war, and criminals, were a form of popular entertainment that captivated Roman citizens. The games were not only a showcase of physical prowess and courage but also a way for the public to participate in the imperial ideology. The presence of the emperor and his involvement in deciding the fate of the gladiators symbolized his ultimate authority and connection with the people.

In addition to gladiatorial combat, the Colosseum hosted venationes, or wild beast hunts, which further emphasized the Romans' domination over the natural world. Exotic animals from the far reaches of the empire were brought to Rome and pitted against each other or against human hunters in displays of raw power and spectacle. These events reinforced the idea of Rome as the center of the known world, with its people as the rulers of all creatures.

The Colosseum also played a significant role in reinforcing social hierarchies. The seating arrangement was a microcosm of Roman society, meticulously organized according to social status. The emperor and the elite sat closest to the action, while women, slaves, and the poor were relegated to the upper tiers. This spatial division reflected the rigid class structure of Roman society and was a daily reminder of one's place within it.

Furthermore, the Colosseum was a venue for public executions, which often staged as dramatic performances. These executions served as a tool for maintaining social order and deterring crime, while also satisfying the public's appetite for spectacle.

In essence, the Colosseum was more than just a venue for entertainment; it was a powerful tool for political propaganda, social control, and cultural expression. It embodied the values of Roman society—valor, power, and order—while providing a space where the empire's might was on full display for all to see. Through its games and spectacles, the Colosseum helped to solidify the collective identity of the Roman people and the supremacy of their civilization.

Fun Facts and Myths

Intriguing Facts

1. **A Wonder of Engineering**: The Colosseum, completed in AD 80, is an engineering marvel of its time. It could hold up to 50,000 spectators and was equipped with a complex system of elevators and trapdoors to facilitate the grand spectacles. These innovations highlight the advanced engineering skills of ancient Romans.

2. **The Name "Colosseum"**: The name "Colosseum" is believed to derive from a colossal statue of Emperor Nero that once stood nearby. Although the statue is long gone, its association with the arena has persisted through the ages.

3. **A Venue for Sea Battles**: The Colosseum was not just a venue for gladiatorial combat; it also hosted naumachiae, or mock sea battles. The arena was specially flooded to reenact naval engagements, showcasing the Romans' ingenuity and their love for grand, theatrical displays.

4. **An Enduring Structure**: Despite being nearly 2,000 years old and suffering from earthquakes,

fires, and stone looting, the Colosseum still stands today. Its enduring presence is a testament to the durability of Roman construction techniques, particularly their use of concrete.

Myths and Legends

1. **The Blood-Soaked Arena**: One of the most enduring myths is that the Colosseum's arena floor absorbed so much blood from the gladiatorial contests that it permanently stained the ground beneath. While it is true that countless animals and gladiators fought to the death, the idea of a blood-soaked arena is more symbolic than literal, representing the brutality of the games.

2. **The Christian Martyr Myth**: Another popular legend is that early Christians were martyred en masse in the Colosseum. While Christians were persecuted in ancient Rome, there is little historical evidence to suggest that the Colosseum was a major site for their execution. This myth, however, has contributed to the Colosseum's image as a place of suffering and sacrifice.

3. **The Curse of the Colosseum**: Some believe that the Colosseum is cursed due to the many lives lost within its walls. This curse is said to bring misfortune to those who disrespect the site, adding an element of supernatural intrigue to the already storied arena.

CHAPTER 1: PLANNING YOUR VISIT

Best Time to Visit

Spring (March to May)

Spring is one of the most pleasant times to visit the Colosseum. The weather is mild, with temperatures ranging from 15°C to 25°C (59°F to 77°F), making it comfortable for exploring not only the Colosseum but also other nearby attractions. The blooming flowers around Rome add to the charm, and the city is not as crowded as it gets in the summer. However, be aware that Easter usually brings an influx of tourists, so it is best to avoid visiting during the Easter weekend if you prefer fewer crowds.

Summer (June to August)

Summer is the peak tourist season in Rome, and the Colosseum sees the highest number of visitors during these months. The weather is hot, often exceeding 30°C (86°F), which can make walking around the ancient structure quite tiring. If you do visit in summer, it's advisable to go early in the morning or late in the afternoon to avoid the midday heat and the largest crowds. Booking tickets in advance is crucial during this time to avoid long lines.

Autumn (September to November)

Autumn is another excellent time to visit the Colosseum. The temperatures begin to cool, ranging from 20°C to 25°C (68°F to 77°F) in September and gradually dropping as you move into November. The crowds begin to thin out after the busy summer months, providing a more relaxed experience. The golden hues of the fall foliage around Rome add a picturesque backdrop to your visit, enhancing the overall experience.

Winter (December to February)

Winter is the least crowded time to visit the Colosseum, making it perfect for those who prefer a quieter atmosphere. Temperatures are cooler, ranging from 5°C to 15°C (41°F to 59°F), and while you might need a warm coat, the lack of crowds means you can take your time exploring the site. The downside is that Rome's winter can be rainy, so be prepared for wet weather. Also, keep in mind that the Colosseum is closed on Christmas Day and New Year's Day.

Recommendation

For the ideal balance of good weather and manageable crowds, the best times to visit the Colosseum are during the shoulder seasons—spring and autumn. These periods offer the most enjoyable conditions for exploring the ancient site without the extreme heat or the overwhelming tourist numbers.

Colosseum Opening Hours

The Colosseum is open to visitors year-round, with opening hours varying slightly depending on the season. For 2024-2025, the general opening hours are as follows:

- **January 2nd to February 15th:** 8:30 AM - 4:30 PM
- **February 16th to March 15th:** 8:30 AM - 5:00 PM
- **March 16th to the last Saturday in March:** 8:30 AM - 5:30 PM
- **From the last Sunday in March to August 31st:** 8:30 AM - 7:15 PM
- **From September 1st through September 30th:** 8:30 AM - 7:00 PM
- **October 1st to the last Saturday in October:** 8:30 AM - 6:30 PM
- **From the last Sunday in October to December 31st:** 8:30 AM - 4:30 PM

Please note that the last admission is one hour before closing time, and the Colosseum is closed on January 1st and December 25th.

Seasonal Variations and Best Times to Visit

The Colosseum's opening hours are adjusted to make the most of daylight hours, especially during the shorter days of winter. In the summer months, the extended hours until 7:15 PM offer ample time for visitors to explore. However, these are also the peak months for tourism, so planning your visit wisely is crucial.

To avoid the heaviest crowds, it's best to visit early in the morning when the Colosseum first opens or later in the afternoon, particularly after 3:00 PM. The morning hours between 8:30 AM and 9:30 AM are generally quieter, allowing you to enjoy the monument with fewer tourists. Alternatively, the late afternoon, especially from 4:00 PM onwards, is another good time to explore, as many tour groups will have already left, and the light begins to soften, creating a beautiful atmosphere.

During the off-peak months from November to February, the Colosseum is less crowded overall, making it an ideal time for those who prefer a more peaceful visit. Even though the opening hours are shorter, the reduced number of visitors allows for a more relaxed experience.

Keep in mind that weekends and public holidays tend to attract more visitors, so if possible, plan your visit on a weekday. For an even more unique experience, consider booking a night tour during the summer, when the Colosseum is beautifully illuminated, offering a different perspective on this ancient structure.

By timing your visit according to these tips, you can make the most of your experience at the Colosseum, avoiding the busiest periods and enjoying the site at its best.

Ticket Information & Prices

Types of Tickets Available

1. **Standard Admission Ticket**: This ticket grants access to the Colosseum, Roman Forum, and Palatine Hill. It is valid for 24 hours from the time of first use, allowing you to explore these historic sites at your own pace. This ticket is perfect for visitors who want a comprehensive experience of ancient Rome.

2. **Full Experience Ticket**: This upgraded option includes all the benefits of the Standard Admission ticket, plus access to special areas of the Colosseum, such as the Arena Floor and the

Underground Chambers. This ticket is ideal for those who want a deeper dive into the Colosseum's history and architecture.

3. **Guided Tour Tickets**: These tickets include a guided tour led by an expert who will share fascinating stories and insights about the Colosseum, Roman Forum, and Palatine Hill. Guided tours are available in various languages and can be an excellent way to enhance your visit.

4. **Night Tour Tickets**: For a unique experience, consider purchasing a Night Tour ticket. These tours allow you to explore the Colosseum under the soft glow of evening lights, offering a different perspective on this iconic monument.

Pricing

- **Standard Admission Ticket**: Prices typically range from €16 to €18, depending on the season.
- **Full Experience Ticket**: Prices are around €25, providing access to additional areas.
- **Guided Tour Tickets**: Prices for guided tours generally start at €30, depending on the tour's length and content.

- **Night Tour Tickets**: Night tours are priced higher, usually around €40 to €50, reflecting the exclusive experience they offer.

Where to Purchase Tickets

Tickets can be purchased in several ways:

- **Official Website**: The most reliable source is the official Colosseum website, which offers tickets without additional fees.
- **Authorized Resellers**: Several authorized online resellers offer tickets, often bundling them with additional services like guided tours.
- **On-Site**: While it's possible to buy tickets at the Colosseum's entrance, it is strongly recommended to purchase them online in advance to avoid long queues and potential sellouts.

Discounts and Special Passes

- **Reduced Price Tickets**: Available for EU citizens aged 18-25, students, and teachers.
- **Free Entry**: Children under 18 and disabled visitors (along with one companion) are eligible for free entry.

- **Roma Pass**: This city pass includes access to the Colosseum, along with other attractions and unlimited public transport for a set number of days.

Guided Tours vs. Self-Guided Tours

Guided Tours: Pros and Cons

Pros:

1. **Expert Insights:** Guided tours provide access to knowledgeable guides who are well-versed in the history, architecture, and cultural significance of the Colosseum. They can offer fascinating stories and lesser-known facts that bring the site to life, enriching your understanding of ancient Rome.

2. **Efficiency:** With a guided tour, you'll follow a well-organized itinerary, ensuring you see all the major highlights without wasting time. Guides know the best routes to avoid crowds, maximizing your time at the site.

3. **Skip-the-Line Access:** Many guided tours include skip-the-line tickets, allowing you to bypass the often long queues at the entrance. This can save you

valuable time, especially during peak tourist seasons.

4. **Interactive Experience:** Some tours offer interactive elements, such as VR experiences or the chance to handle replica artifacts. These additions can make your visit more engaging and memorable.

Cons:

1. **Cost:** Guided tours tend to be more expensive than self-guided visits. The added value of a guide and skip-the-line access comes at a premium, which might not fit every traveler's budget.

2. **Less Flexibility:** On a guided tour, you'll need to stick to a set schedule. This means less freedom to explore areas that interest you the most or spend additional time in sections of the Colosseum that captivate you.

Self-Guided Tours: Pros and Cons

Pros:

1. **Flexibility:** Exploring on your own gives you the freedom to set your own pace. You can linger in areas that fascinate you or skip parts that are less

interesting, tailoring your visit to your personal preferences.

2. **Cost-Effective:** Self-guided tours are usually cheaper, as you only need to purchase an entry ticket. If you are on a budget, this can be a more economical option.

3. **Personal Experience:** Without a guide, you can experience the Colosseum in a more personal and introspective way, allowing you to connect with the site in your own time and manner.

Cons:

1. **Missed Information:** Without a guide, you may miss out on important historical context and intriguing details that bring the Colosseum's history to life. While audio guides and guidebooks can help, they may not offer the same depth as a live guide.

2. **Potential for Overwhelm:** The Colosseum is vast, and without guidance, it can be easy to miss key areas or feel overwhelmed by the sheer amount of information available.

Accessibility Information

Mobility Accessibility

The Colosseum is partially wheelchair accessible. The main entrance is equipped with ramps, allowing easy access for visitors using wheelchairs or those with limited mobility. The ground floor, which includes most of the key sections such as the arena and some exhibits, is fully accessible. However, the upper levels of the Colosseum, which offer expansive views of the interior and the surrounding area, are not wheelchair accessible due to the steep and uneven staircases.

For those who require assistance, there are wheelchairs available at the entrance, which can be requested upon arrival. It is advisable to contact the Colosseum in advance to ensure availability and to discuss any specific needs.

Visual and Hearing Impairments

Visitors with visual or hearing impairments can also enjoy a fulfilling experience at the Colosseum. Audio guides are available and include detailed descriptions of the site's history and key features. These guides can be paired with personal devices or headphones to accommodate hearing aids. Additionally, some guided tours offer sign language interpretation or can be adapted to include more detailed verbal descriptions for visually impaired visitors.

For those who prefer a tactile experience, there are models of the Colosseum available on-site that can be touched, providing a sense of the structure's layout and dimensions. Information panels around the Colosseum are also equipped with Braille descriptions.

Restrooms and Facilities

Accessible restrooms are available within the Colosseum complex, located near the entrance and in various sections throughout the site. These restrooms are designed to accommodate wheelchairs and include support bars and emergency call buttons.

Assistance and Support

The Colosseum staff are trained to assist visitors with disabilities. If you need help during your visit, staff members are readily available to provide assistance or answer any questions. It is recommended to arrive early or during less crowded times to ensure a smoother experience.

Advance Booking and Special Arrangements

To enhance your visit, it is advisable to book tickets in advance and inform the Colosseum of any special requirements. This allows the staff to prepare and ensure that all necessary accommodations are in place.

While the Colosseum's ancient structure does present some accessibility challenges, the site has made considerable efforts to welcome all visitors and ensure that everyone can experience the grandeur of this historic landmark.

CHAPTER 2: GETTING THERE

Directions from Rome's Airports

From Fiumicino Airport (Leonardo da Vinci)

Fiumicino is Rome's main international airport and is approximately 30 kilometers (18 miles) from the city center. To reach the Colosseum, you have several options:

1. **Leonardo Express Train**: The Leonardo Express is the fastest and most convenient way to reach the city center. Trains depart every 15-30 minutes from the airport and take about 32 minutes to arrive at Roma Termini, Rome's central train station. From Roma Termini, take Metro Line B (blue line) toward Laurentina and get off at the second stop, Colosseo. The Colosseum is just outside the metro station.

2. **Regional FL1 Train**: A more economical option, the FL1 train runs every 15 minutes and stops at several stations within Rome. However, it does not go to Roma Termini. To reach the Colosseum, take the FL1 train to Roma Ostiense station, and then

transfer to Metro Line B toward Rebibbia or Jonio. Get off at Colosseo.

3. **Taxi or Private Transfer**: Taxis are available outside the airport terminals, with a fixed fare of around €50 to the city center. Ensure the taxi is official (white with a taxi sign). Private transfers can also be pre-booked for a more comfortable and direct journey. The ride to the Colosseum typically takes about 40-60 minutes, depending on traffic.

4. **Bus Services**: Several bus companies operate services from Fiumicino to Roma Termini, including Terravision and SIT Bus Shuttle. The journey takes about 45-60 minutes. From Termini, follow the directions mentioned above to reach the Colosseum via Metro Line B.

From Ciampino Airport

Ciampino is Rome's secondary airport, located about 15 kilometers (9 miles) southeast of the city center. Here's how to reach the Colosseum:

1. **Bus to Metro**: The most straightforward route is to take a shuttle bus (such as the Terravision or SIT Bus Shuttle) from Ciampino Airport to Roma

Termini. The bus journey takes around 40 minutes. From Termini, take Metro Line B toward Laurentina and alight at Colosseo.

2. **Taxi or Private Transfer**: Taxis from Ciampino to the city center cost around €30, with the journey to the Colosseum taking 30-40 minutes. As always, make sure to use official taxis or pre-arrange a private transfer for a hassle-free experience.

3. **Bus to Anagnina Metro Station**: A budget-friendly option is to take a local bus from the airport to Anagnina, the southern terminus of Metro Line A (orange line). The bus ride takes about 15 minutes. From Anagnina, take Metro Line A toward Battistini and transfer to Line B at Termini. Continue on Line B to Colosseo.

Public Transportation Options

Metro

The Colosseum is directly accessible via the Rome Metro on Line B (the Blue Line). The closest station is **Colosseo**, which is right across the street from the Colosseum's entrance. As you exit the station, you'll be greeted by an awe-inspiring view of the monument. The metro is often the fastest option, especially if you are traveling from other major sites or neighborhoods within Rome. Trains run frequently, with peak service intervals as short as every 3 minutes during rush hours.

For those coming from central areas like Termini Station, you can take Line B directly to Colosseo in just two stops. If you are staying near the Vatican or other parts of Rome served by Line A, you can easily transfer to Line B at Termini.

Buses

Several bus routes stop near the Colosseum, providing a scenic way to travel through the city. The most convenient lines include:

- **75:** Runs from the Trastevere area, passing through key locations such as Termini Station before arriving at the Colosseum.
- **81:** Connects the Vatican area to the Colosseum, passing through the historic center, including Piazza Venezia.
- **673:** Provides a quick route from the San Giovanni area, with stops near the Colosseum.

Buses in Rome are generally reliable, but they can be slower during peak hours due to traffic. However, they offer the advantage of seeing more of the city above ground, making them a good option if you prefer to take in the sights as you travel.

Trams

The tram system in Rome is another option, though it does not have a stop directly at the Colosseum. The nearest tram stop is **Piazza del Colosseo**, served by Tram Line 3. This line runs through areas such as Trastevere, Testaccio, and the Villa Borghese area, providing a scenic route that ends just a short walk from the Colosseum.

Tips for Using Public Transport

Rome's public transport operates on a unified ticket system. You can purchase tickets at metro stations, newsstands, or tobacco shops (tabaccherie). Be sure to validate your ticket upon boarding to avoid fines. If you plan to use public transport frequently, consider purchasing a day pass for unlimited travel.

Parking Facilities Nearby

Public Parking Garages

One of the most reliable options for parking near the Colosseum is using public parking garages. These garages are secure and conveniently located, though they can be a bit pricey.

- **Parcheggio Colosseo (Piazza del Colosseo):** Located just a few minutes' walk from the Colosseum, this underground parking facility offers a convenient option for those wanting to be as close as possible. It's ideal for short visits but be prepared for higher rates due to its prime location.

- **Parcheggio Via Ostilia (Via Ostilia 48):** Another nearby parking garage, Parcheggio Via Ostilia, is a bit further from the Colosseum but offers slightly lower rates. It's a good balance between proximity and cost.

- **Parcheggio San Giovanni (Piazza San Giovanni in Laterano):** Although a bit farther from the Colosseum, this parking garage is near the San Giovanni Metro station, making it easy to park and take public transport directly to the Colosseum.

Street Parking

Street parking in the area surrounding the Colosseum can be challenging due to high demand and strict regulations. However, if you prefer this option, here are a few tips:

- **Blue Lines:** Look for blue-lined spaces, which indicate paid street parking. These spaces are metered, and payment can be made at nearby machines or via a mobile app. Be sure to check the signs for hours of operation and time limits.
- **White Lines:** These spaces indicate free parking, but they are scarce and usually fill up quickly. Be cautious of restrictions, as some white-lined spaces may be reserved for residents only.

- **Parking Time Limits:** Many street parking spots near the Colosseum have time limits, so be aware of how long you can park to avoid fines.

Tips for Parking Near the Colosseum

- **Arrive Early:** If you plan to visit during peak tourist season or on weekends, arriving early increases your chances of finding a good parking spot.

- **Consider Alternative Transport:** Given the challenges of driving and parking in central Rome, you might find it easier to park further away and take public transport or a taxi to the Colosseum.

- **Use Parking Apps:** Several parking apps can help you find available spots and pay for parking. This can help conserve time and alleviate stress.

CHAPTER 3: EXPLORING THE COLOSSEUM

Must-See Highlights

1. The Arena Floor

The heart of the Colosseum, the arena floor, is where the brutal gladiatorial contests and spectacles took place. Although much of the original floor is gone, standing on the reconstructed section gives visitors a powerful sense of the scale and intensity of the events that once captivated Roman audiences. From here, you can imagine the roar of the crowd and the tension of life-or-death battles that made the Colosseum famous.

2. The Underground Chambers (Hypogeum)

Beneath the arena floor lies the Hypogeum, a labyrinth of tunnels and chambers that housed the gladiators, animals, and stage machinery used in the spectacles. This area is a testament to the advanced engineering of ancient Rome, with complex pulley systems and trapdoors that allowed for dramatic entrances during the games. Exploring the Hypogeum reveals the behind-the-scenes workings of the Colosseum, providing a deeper understanding of the logistics and preparation involved in staging the grand spectacles.

3. The Upper Levels

The upper levels of the Colosseum offer panoramic views of the structure itself and the surrounding city of Rome. These levels, which once seated the common citizens of Rome, provide a unique perspective on the sheer size and architectural brilliance of the amphitheater. From here, visitors can appreciate the Colosseum's role as both a marvel of engineering and a central gathering place for the people of ancient Rome.

4. The Arch of Constantine Viewpoint

Located just outside the Colosseum, the Arch of Constantine is a triumphal arch that commemorates Emperor Constantine's victory at the Battle of Milvian Bridge. While not technically part of the Colosseum, this nearby attraction is often included in the visit. The viewpoint from the Colosseum offers a perfect spot to admire this majestic structure, symbolizing Rome's transition from a pagan to a Christian empire.

5. *The Outer Façade and Archways:*

The Colosseum's exterior is a masterpiece of Roman architecture, with its towering arches and intricate details. The façade, made from travertine stone, once gleamed in the Roman sunlight, and even today, its imposing structure inspires awe. Walking around the exterior, visitors can see the remains of the original statues and inscriptions that adorned the archways, offering a glimpse into the grandeur that once was.

Interactive Exhibits & Displays

Virtual Reality Experience

One of the most popular interactive experiences is the Virtual Reality (VR) tour. This cutting-edge technology allows visitors to step back in time and witness the Colosseum as it once was, in all its glory. Wearing VR headsets, guests are transported to ancient Rome, where they can explore a fully reconstructed Colosseum, complete with roaring crowds, gladiatorial combat, and even the intricate underground network that housed animals and slaves. This immersive experience not only provides a visual feast but also a deeper understanding of the

Colosseum's role in Roman society and the sheer scale of events that took place within its walls.

Interactive Touchscreens

Scattered throughout the Colosseum are interactive touchscreens that offer detailed information about the various sections of the amphitheater. These displays provide a mix of historical data, 3D models, and multimedia content, allowing visitors to explore the Colosseum's architectural details and learn about its construction techniques. For example, visitors can interact with a touchscreen to see how the massive stones were moved into place, how the complex system of trapdoors and pulleys operated, and how the arena could be flooded for naval battles. These interactive elements cater to all types of learners, making the history accessible and engaging for both adults and children.

Augmented Reality (AR) Displays

Augmented Reality (AR) displays add another layer of engagement by overlaying digital reconstructions onto the Colosseum's ruins. Using tablets or smartphones, visitors can see how the Colosseum's exterior and interior appeared in its prime, with superimposed images showing where statues, arches, and other architectural features were located. This AR experience not only enriches the visual experience but also helps visitors appreciate the scale and grandeur of the Colosseum as it once stood.

Educational Exhibits

In addition to these digital experiences, the Colosseum also features traditional educational exhibits that delve into various aspects of Roman life and culture. These exhibits often include interactive elements such as replicas of gladiator weapons and armor that visitors can touch and examine. Additionally, there are displays that explain the social hierarchy of the spectators, the types of events held, and the engineering marvels that allowed the Colosseum to function as a massive entertainment venue.

Photography Tips

Best Spots for Photography

1. **The Arena Floor:** The Arena floor offers a unique perspective, allowing you to photograph the towering walls from below. This angle highlights the scale and architectural details of the Colosseum.

Try to capture the sunlight streaming through the arches, which adds dramatic lighting to your shots.

2. **The Upper Levels:** The upper levels provide panoramic views of the entire structure, as well as the surrounding Roman Forum and Palatine Hill. From here, you can capture wide-angle shots that encompass the Colosseum's full scale. For an even more expansive view, use a panoramic mode on your camera or smartphone.

3. **The Outer Archways:** The archways on the exterior of the Colosseum are perfect for framing your shots. Use the arches to create natural frames for the interior or the distant views of Rome. This technique adds depth to your photos and emphasizes the Colosseum's iconic architecture.

4. **The Underground Chambers:** Although dimly lit, the underground chambers offer a chance to capture the mysterious and ancient atmosphere of the Colosseum. Use a higher ISO setting or bring a tripod to stabilize your camera for longer exposures. Focus on the textures and the play of light and shadow in these historical spaces.

Best Time of Day for Photography

- **Early Morning:** Visiting the Colosseum early in the morning, just after it opens, is ideal for photographers. The crowds are minimal, and the soft, golden light of the early hours enhances the warm tones of the stone. This is also the best time to capture the exterior of the Colosseum without too many tourists in your shots.

- **Late Afternoon/Golden Hour:** The golden hour, just before sunset, is another excellent time for photography. The warm, slanting sunlight adds a golden hue to the stone, creating a beautiful contrast between light and shadow. This time of day also provides a softer light that is less harsh than midday sun, making it easier to capture detailed shots without overexposure.

- **Nighttime:** For a different perspective, consider photographing the Colosseum at night. The monument is beautifully illuminated, casting a glow that makes for dramatic and atmospheric photos. A long exposure can create stunning effects, capturing the light trails of passing cars with the Colosseum as a majestic backdrop.

CHAPTER 4: SPECIAL EXPERIENCES

Night Tours of the Colosseum

Experiencing the Colosseum under the cloak of night is a journey into the heart of ancient Rome like no other. As the sun sets and the day's crowds dissipate, the Colosseum transforms into a serene, almost mystical monument, bathed in soft, ambient lighting that accentuates its ancient arches and towering walls. The atmosphere during a night tour is profoundly different from the bustling energy of the daytime, offering a more intimate and contemplative exploration of this historic site.

The night tour begins as you step into the Colosseum, greeted by the cool evening air and the gentle hum of the city in the background. The grandeur of the illuminated amphitheater against the dark sky creates a dramatic contrast that evokes a sense of awe and reverence. The play of light and shadow across the ancient stonework brings out details that are often overlooked in the harsh daylight, allowing visitors to appreciate the architectural genius of this nearly 2,000-year-old structure.

One of the most striking differences during a night tour is the silence. Without the throngs of daytime visitors, the Colosseum feels almost sacred, as if the echoes of history are more present in the stillness. This quietude allows for a more personal connection with the space, where the imagination can run free, conjuring images of the gladiators who once fought here, the roar of the ancient crowds, and the pageantry of imperial Rome.

Night tours also offer exclusive access to areas that are not always available during the day. The underground chambers, where gladiators and wild animals were once kept before battles, are often included in these tours, providing a glimpse into the behind-the-scenes workings of the Colosseum. Walking through these dimly lit tunnels, you can almost feel the weight of history, as if stepping back in time to the days of the Roman Empire.

The reduced number of visitors on night tours ensures that the experience is more leisurely and less hurried. Guides have the opportunity to delve deeper into the stories and legends of the Colosseum, creating a narrative that is both educational and immersive. Whether you are a history buff or simply seeking a unique way to experience one of the world's most iconic landmarks, a night tour of the Colosseum is an unforgettable journey into the past.

Virtual Reality and Augmented Reality Experiences

Technology Behind VR and AR Experiences

VR experiences at the Colosseum utilize headsets that fully immerse visitors in a digitally reconstructed environment of ancient Rome. As visitors wear the VR headset, they are transported back in time, witnessing the Colosseum as it once stood, with its towering arches, bustling crowds, and intense gladiatorial combats. The technology creates a 360-degree view, allowing users to look around as if they were physically present in ancient times. These VR experiences often include guided narratives, providing historical context and highlighting key aspects of the Colosseum's architecture and social significance.

On the other hand, AR experiences use smartphone apps or AR glasses to overlay digital information onto the real-world view of the Colosseum. As visitors explore the site, they can point their device at various features, triggering animations, reconstructions, or informative text that appears on their screen. This technology allows visitors to see how specific parts of the Colosseum looked in their original form, offering a deeper understanding of its structure and purpose.

Enhancing Visitor Understanding

Both VR and AR experiences significantly enhance a visitor's understanding of the Colosseum by bringing its history to life in ways that static displays and traditional tours cannot. These technologies allow visitors to visualize the grandeur of the Colosseum in its prime, providing a sense of scale and atmosphere that is difficult to grasp from the ruins alone.

Through VR, visitors can experience a gladiatorial fight or the roar of a 50,000-strong crowd, helping them understand the sheer magnitude and cultural importance of the events that took place here. The immersive nature of VR makes history feel tangible, engaging the senses and emotions in a way that deepens learning and retention.

AR, meanwhile, acts as a virtual tour guide, offering contextual information exactly when and where it is needed. By overlaying digital reconstructions onto the existing ruins, AR helps visitors connect the dots between the Colosseum's present state and its historical past, making the experience more meaningful and informative.

Gladiator Experience Tours

The "Gladiator Experience" is an immersive journey that transports participants back to the days of ancient Rome, offering a unique opportunity to walk in the footsteps of the Colosseum's legendary warriors. These tours are designed to be both educational and interactive, making history come alive in a way that standard tours cannot.

What to Expect

Participants typically begin their experience with a guided tour of the Colosseum, where they receive an overview of the history and significance of gladiatorial combat in Roman culture. This initial tour sets the stage, providing context about the lives of gladiators, their training, and the brutal spectacles that once entertained thousands.

Interactive Gladiator Training

The highlight of the Gladiator Experience is the training session, often held at an authentic gladiator school (ludus) near the Colosseum or at a specially designed area within the Colosseum itself. Participants are outfitted in replica gladiatorial gear, including tunics, helmets, and wooden training swords (rudis). Under the guidance of expert instructors, who often portray seasoned gladiators or Roman soldiers, participants learn the basic combat techniques and strategies used in ancient times.

The training covers various aspects, including:

- **Weaponry Handling**: Learning how to wield different types of gladiatorial weapons, from swords and shields to tridents and nets.

- **Combat Stances and Moves**: Practicing the defensive and offensive moves that gladiators would have mastered to survive in the arena.

- **Tactical Training**: Understanding the importance of strategy and adapting to different opponents, much like the gladiators who faced a variety of adversaries in the Colosseum.

The instructors, knowledgeable in both history and martial arts, ensure that the training is safe and enjoyable, while also providing insights into the physical and mental challenges faced by the gladiators.

The Arena Experience

Depending on the tour, participants may also have the chance to simulate a gladiatorial combat scenario in a mock arena, complete with a cheering crowd (sometimes other participants). This part of the experience allows participants to put their newly acquired skills to the test in a controlled and entertaining environment, offering a small taste of what it might have felt like to fight for survival and glory.

Learning Outcomes

Beyond the physical activity, the Gladiator Experience offers a deeper understanding of the social and cultural dynamics of ancient Rome. Participants leave with a greater appreciation for the gladiators' role in Roman society, the brutality of the games, and the engineering marvel that is the Colosseum.

Special Events & Seasonal Shows

Night Tours and Light Shows

One of the most enchanting experiences at the Colosseum is the *"La Luna sul Colosseo"* (Moon over the Colosseum) night tour. Available from spring through early autumn, this guided tour allows visitors to explore the Colosseum under the soft glow of the moon. The tour includes access to areas typically closed to the public during the day, such as the underground chambers where gladiators and animals awaited their fates. Atmospheric lighting and storytelling, bringing the Colosseum's history to life in a way that is both eerie and captivating, heighten the experience.

During select times of the year, the Colosseum also hosts spectacular light shows, where its ancient stones become the canvas for projections that narrate the building's history. These multimedia displays combine light, sound, and imagery, offering a breathtaking visual journey through time. Visitors planning to experience these light shows should check the official Colosseum website for dates and ticket availability, as these events are popular and often sell out quickly.

Historical Reenactments

On certain dates, particularly around Rome's birthday in April (Natale di Roma), the Colosseum becomes the stage for historical reenactments. These events often include mock gladiator battles, traditional Roman ceremonies, and parades featuring participants dressed as Roman soldiers, senators, and citizens. These reenactments offer a vivid glimpse into the past, allowing visitors to witness the type of spectacles that once entertained ancient Romans. Planning a visit during these events can enhance the educational and entertainment value of the trip.

Seasonal Art Installations and Exhibitions

The Colosseum frequently hosts temporary art installations and exhibitions, often in collaboration with contemporary artists and historians. These exhibits are typically located in the outer areas of the Colosseum or in the Roman Forum and Palatine Hill complex. They provide a modern interpretation of ancient history, connecting the past with the present. These exhibitions rotate throughout the year, so it's worth checking the schedule ahead of your visit.

Planning Your Visit

To make the most of these special events and shows, it's crucial to plan your visit accordingly. Always check the Colosseum's official website or local tourist information centers for the latest schedules and ticket information. Booking in advance is highly recommended, especially during peak tourist seasons or for events that have limited availability. By aligning your visit with one of these special events, you can experience the Colosseum in a truly unforgettable way.

CHAPTER 5: PRACTICAL INFORMATION

Security Procedures & Bag Checks

Security Screening Process

Upon arrival at the Colosseum, all visitors are required to pass through a security checkpoint. This process is similar to airport security and involves passing through metal detectors. Visitors should be prepared to remove items such as belts, watches, and metallic objects from their pockets before going through the detectors. Security personnel may also use hand-held scanners to conduct additional checks if needed.

Bag Checks

Security staff at the entrance will inspect all bags, backpacks, and personal belongings. To expedite the process and avoid delays, it is recommended that visitors bring only small bags. Large backpacks, luggage, and bulky items are not permitted inside the Colosseum and should be left at your accommodation or in a secure storage facility before your visit. Additionally, there are no storage facilities available on-site, so plan accordingly.

Prohibited Items

For the safety of all visitors, certain items are strictly prohibited inside the Colosseum. These include:

- Weapons of any type, including knives and firearms.
- Sharp objects, such as scissors and tools
- Explosive materials, fireworks, and flammable liquids
- Large umbrellas with pointed tips (small, foldable umbrellas are allowed)
- Glass bottles, cans, and alcohol
- Drones and remote-controlled devices
- Professional camera equipment, such as tripods and selfie sticks, unless special permission has been obtained
- Food and drinks, except for small bottles of water (Note: There are water fountains available inside)

Expected Wait Times

Given the popularity of the Colosseum, expect some wait times at the security checkpoint, especially during peak tourist seasons. To minimize wait times, consider arriving early in the morning or later in the afternoon. Be patient and follow the instructions of security personnel to ensure a smooth entry.

Additional Tips

To ensure a hassle-free visit, it is advisable to check the Colosseum's official website or contact their visitor services for any updates on security procedures or prohibited items before your visit. Being informed and prepared will help you navigate the security checks efficiently, allowing you more time to enjoy the awe-inspiring experience of exploring the Colosseum.

What to Wear & Bring

Clothing Tips

- **Comfortable Footwear:** The Colosseum is vast, with uneven surfaces, ancient stones, and stairs to navigate. Opt for sturdy, comfortable shoes with good grip, such as walking shoes or sneakers. Avoid heels or sandals that might not provide enough support.
- **Seasonal Attire:**

o **Spring and Fall:** These are the best seasons to visit, with mild weather. Light layers are ideal—think a breathable t-shirt with a light jacket or sweater. Mornings and evenings can be cool, so having an extra layer handy is advisable.

o **Summer:** Rome's summer temperatures can soar above 90°F (32°C). Lightweight, breathable clothing is essential. Choose light-colored fabrics like cotton or linen to stay cool. A wide-brimmed hat and sunglasses will help protect you from the strong sun. Consider wearing moisture-wicking clothing to stay comfortable.

o **Winter:** Winters in Rome are generally mild, but it can get chilly, especially in the early morning or late afternoon. It is advisable to wear a warm coat, along with a scarf and gloves. Layering your clothing is essential, as it enables you to adapt to varying temperatures.

- **Respectful Dress:** While the Colosseum is an outdoor attraction, it is also a site of great historical significance. Dress respectfully, avoiding overly revealing clothing. If you plan to visit nearby churches or religious sites, keep in mind that shoulders and knees should be covered.

Essentials to Bring

- **Water Bottle:** Hydration is crucial, especially in the summer heat. Bring a refillable water bottle; there are public fountains nearby where you can refill.
- **Sun Protection:** Sunscreen is necessary, even on cloudy days, to protect your skin from UV rays. A lightweight, portable umbrella can also serve as sun protection.
- **Day Pack:** A small backpack or crossbody bag is ideal for carrying your essentials. Choose one that is secure and easy to carry, as you will be on your feet a lot.
- **Portable Charger:** The Colosseum offers plenty of photo opportunities. Ensure your phone or camera stays charged by bringing a portable charger.

- **Light Snacks:** While food is not allowed inside the Colosseum, having a snack handy for before or after your visit can be useful, especially if you plan to explore the surrounding area.

Food & Drink Options Nearby

1. La Taverna dei Fori Imperiali

Just a 10-minute walk from the Colosseum, this family-run trattoria is a beloved spot for both locals and tourists. La Taverna dei Fori Imperiali offers a cozy atmosphere and a menu full of Roman classics like **Cacio e Pepe**, **Carbonara**, and **Saltimbocca alla Romana**. The authenticity of the food and the warm hospitality make it a must-visit for an authentic Roman dining experience.

2. Aroma Restaurant

For those seeking a fine dining experience with an unforgettable view, Aroma Restaurant, located on the rooftop of the Palazzo Manfredi Hotel, is the perfect choice. Overlooking the Colosseum, this Michelin-starred restaurant offers a contemporary take on Italian cuisine. Dishes like **risotto with saffron and licorice** or **veal cheek with Jerusalem artichokes** are crafted with precision and creativity, making it an ideal spot for a special occasion.

3. Trattoria Luzzi

A more budget-friendly option, Trattoria Luzzi, is a popular spot for locals and travelers alike. Just a stone's throw from the Colosseum, Luzzi serves hearty portions of traditional Roman dishes at reasonable prices. Their wood-fired pizzas and house-made pasta dishes like **Amatriciana** and **Gricia** are particularly popular, offering a true taste of Roman comfort food.

4. Gelateria La Dolce Vita

No trip to Rome is complete without indulging in gelato, and Gelateria La Dolce Vita, located near the Colosseum, is the perfect place to satisfy your sweet tooth. Offering a wide range of flavors, from traditional **Pistachio** and **Stracciatella** to more adventurous choices like **Ricotta and Figs**, this gelateria is a great spot for a refreshing treat after exploring the ancient ruins.

5. Oppio Caffè

For a casual coffee break or a quick snack, Oppio Caffè, located in front of the Colosseum on via delle Terme di Tito, provides a fantastic view of the monument. Whether you are grabbing a quick **espresso** or enjoying a light lunch with a **Panini** or **salad**, the outdoor seating makes it a perfect spot to relax while taking in the historic surroundings.

Restroom Locations

Inside the Colosseum

The main restrooms within the Colosseum are located near the entrance on the ground floor, close to the ticket check area. These facilities are generally well-maintained and accessible. However, during peak hours, especially in the late morning and early afternoon, lines can form. To avoid long waits, consider using these restrooms early in the morning when you first enter, or later in the afternoon when crowds begin to thin out.

Outside the Colosseum

If the lines inside are long, you can find additional restrooms just outside the Colosseum. One of the most convenient options is located near the Arch of Constantine, which is just a short walk from the Colosseum's main entrance. These restrooms are often less crowded, making them a good alternative during busy periods.

Nearby Cafés and Restaurants

Another option is to visit a nearby café or restaurant. Establishments in the vicinity, especially along Via di San

Gregorio and Via dei Fori Imperiali, typically allow customers to use their restrooms. If you are planning to stop for a coffee or a quick bite, this can be a convenient way to use a restroom without the wait. Just be aware that some places may require a small purchase to access their facilities.

Tips for Avoiding Long Lines

1. **Timing:** As mentioned, the best way to avoid long lines is to use the restrooms early in the morning or late in the afternoon. Crowds peak between 10 a.m. and 2 p.m., so plan accordingly.

2. **Off-Peak Visits:** If possible, plan your visit during off-peak days, such as weekdays outside of the high tourist season. The reduced number of visitors generally means shorter lines for restrooms.

3. **Alternative Facilities:** If you are exploring nearby attractions, such as the Roman Forum or Palatine Hill, consider using the restrooms at these sites before or after your visit to the Colosseum. These areas are part of the same complex and may offer less crowded facilities.

Lost & Found Information

Immediate Steps after Realizing an Item is Lost

1. **Retrace Your Steps:** As soon as you realize something is missing, try to retrace your steps within the Colosseum. Sometimes, the item might be nearby where you last had it, especially in less crowded areas.

2. **Alert a Staff Member:** If you cannot locate the item after a quick search, immediately notify the nearest Colosseum staff member. Staff are trained to assist with lost items and can provide guidance on what to do next. They may direct you to the Colosseum's main Lost & Found office or help you file a report.

3. **Visit the Lost & Found Office:** The Colosseum has a dedicated Lost & Found office where found items are catalogued and stored temporarily. The office is usually located near the main entrance or exit, making it convenient for visitors. You may need to provide a description of the lost item and the approximate time and place you lost it.

What to Provide

When reporting a lost item, be ready to give specific details to help identify your belongings:

- **Item Description:** Be as detailed as possible when describing the lost item. Include the color, brand, size, and any unique features that distinguish it.
- **Time and Location:** Mention the last time and place you remember having the item. This information can help staff narrow down the search area.
- **Contact Information:** Leave your contact details with the Lost & Found office so they can reach you if your item is found later.

Follow-Up

If your item is not immediately found, do not lose hope. The Colosseum is Lost & Found office maintains a log of all items turned in and regularly updates their records. You may need to follow up with the office in person or by phone in the following days. It is also a good idea to check your email or phone regularly, as they may contact you if your item is found after you have left the site.

If you have Already Left Rome

For visitors who have already left Rome, you can still inquire about lost items by contacting the Colosseum's Lost & Found office via phone or email. If your item is located, you may be able to arrange for it to be mailed back to you, though you might be responsible for any shipping costs. While losing an item is unfortunate, the Colosseum staff are there to assist you in every way possible, ensuring your visit remains memorable for all the right reasons.

CHAPTER 6: UNDERSTANDING THE HISTORY

The Construction of the Colosseum

The Colosseum, also known as the Flavian Amphitheater, stands as a testament to the architectural and engineering brilliance of ancient Rome. Its construction, which began under Emperor Vespasian around 70-72 AD and was completed in 80 AD under his son Titus, showcases the Romans' mastery of large-scale building projects and their ability to combine functionality with grandeur.

Materials and Structure

The Colosseum was primarily constructed from a combination of travertine limestone, tuff (a type of volcanic rock), and concrete. The outer walls were made of travertine, a durable material sourced from nearby quarries in Tivoli. This stone provided both strength and an aesthetic appeal with its warm, golden hue. Tuff was used in the internal structure, providing a lighter, more flexible material that was easier to work with and supported the massive weight of the upper tiers. Roman concrete, a mixture of lime mortar, volcanic ash, and aggregates, was a revolutionary material that allowed for the construction of the Colosseum's intricate vaults and arches.

Engineering Techniques

The Colosseum's architecture stands as a remarkable feat of Roman engineering. The elliptical shape of the amphitheater, measuring 189 meters long and 156 meters wide, was not only aesthetically pleasing but also structurally sound, distributing weight evenly across its foundations. The structure's four levels could accommodate over 50,000 spectators, with each level supported by a series of arches, creating a balanced distribution of weight and enabling the construction of the towering 48-meter-high facade.

One of the most impressive engineering feats was the extensive use of vaults and arches throughout the Colosseum. The Romans employed a series of barrel vaults to support the seating areas, while the exterior was adorned with three tiers of 80 arches, providing both stability and a method of crowd control. These arches also allowed for the insertion of large entrances and exits, enabling the swift movement of people in and out of the amphitheater.

Innovative Features

The Colosseum also featured a complex underground network known as the hypogeum, which included a series of tunnels, chambers, and elevators used to house gladiators, animals, and stage props. This subterranean level was a masterpiece of engineering, complete with trapdoors and lifts operated by a pulley system, allowing for dramatic entrances during events.

The Significance of the Colosseum in Ancient Roman Society

The Colosseum, or Flavian Amphitheatre, was far more than just a grand architectural marvel; it was a powerful symbol of the social and political dynamics of ancient Rome. Constructed under Emperor Vespasian and completed by his son Titus in 80 AD, the Colosseum quickly became the epicenter of public life, reflecting the values, priorities, and complexities of Roman society.

Social Role: The Arena of the People

The Colosseum was a stage where the social hierarchy of Rome was both upheld and blurred. With a seating capacity of up to 50,000 spectators, the amphitheater hosted a wide array of public spectacles, including gladiatorial contests, animal hunts, and dramatic reenactments of famous battles. These events were free to the public, a testament to the concept of *bread and circuses* (panem et circenses), where the emperors sought to placate and entertain the populace, thus securing their favor and minimizing social unrest.

Seating arrangements within the Colosseum were a direct reflection of the rigid class structure in Roman society. The emperor and the elite occupied the best seats closest to the action, while women, slaves, and the poor were relegated to the higher tiers. Despite this, the shared experience of watching the games allowed for a rare moment of unity, where Romans of all classes gathered to witness the grandeur of their empire.

Political Role: Power and Propaganda

Politically, the Colosseum was a tool of immense power and propaganda. Emperors used the games as a means to display their generosity and reinforce their status as benefactors of the Roman people. The elaborate spectacles, often paid for by the emperor himself, served to demonstrate the wealth, military prowess, and divine favor of the ruling class.

The games also functioned as a political theater where the might of the Roman Empire was showcased. Gladiators, often prisoners of war, symbolized Rome's dominance over its enemies. The public execution of criminals and the reenactment of famous military victories reinforced the idea of Roman justice and the superiority of Roman culture.

Reflection of Values and Priorities

The Colosseum's role in ancient Rome highlighted the values of strength, discipline, and public order, which were central to Roman identity. It celebrated martial prowess, the subjugation of enemies, and the ability of the state to provide for and entertain its people. The massive scale of the building and the grandeur of the events it hosted were a reflection of Rome's priorities: maintaining social cohesion through public spectacle, promoting the glory of the empire, and reinforcing the authority of the emperor.

In essence, the Colosseum was a microcosm of Roman society—an arena where the power dynamics, social structures, and cultural values of one of history's greatest empires were vividly on display.

Gladiators: Life and Battles

Life of a Gladiator

Gladiators were usually slaves, prisoners of war, or criminals sentenced to fight in the arena. However, some free men volunteered, drawn by the potential for fame, fortune, or simply the thrill of battle. Life for a gladiator was brutal and harsh. They lived in schools called *ludi*, where they trained relentlessly under the watchful eyes of a *lanista*, the owner and trainer of gladiators. Despite their low status, gladiators were well fed and given medical care to ensure, they were in peak physical condition for the arena.

Training Regimen

Training for gladiators was intense and rigorous. Each gladiator specialized in a particular fighting style, often determined by the type of weapon and armor they used. For example, a *retiarius* fought with a net and trident, relying on speed and agility, while a *murmillo* wielded a sword and shield, emphasizing strength and endurance. Training involved mock combat, conditioning exercises, and learning tactics to exploit their opponents' weaknesses. Gladiators also practiced in groups, honing their skills in various formations that mimicked real battle scenarios.

The Battles

Gladiatorial battles were not mere chaotic brawls; they were highly choreographed and strategic contests. The arena's organizers, who paired fighters of different styles to create a dramatic and thrilling spectacle, carefully curated each match. The audience, often including the Emperor, played a significant role in these events. They cheered, booed, and sometimes even decided the fate of the defeated gladiator by signalling for mercy or death with a thumbs-up or thumbs-down gesture.

For the gladiators, the battles were a matter of survival, but they also carried deeper significance. These fights were not just entertainment but a demonstration of Roman virtues like *virtus* (courage) and *dignitas* (honor). A gladiator's ability to fight with skill and die with dignity was a testament to these values, earning them the respect of the crowd, and sometimes even their freedom. Victorious gladiators could become celebrities, immortalized in art and rewarded with wealth and adoration, though few lived to enjoy these spoils for long.

The Decline and Preservation Efforts

The Colosseum, once the grandest amphitheater in ancient Rome, has endured a long and tumultuous journey of decline and revival. After the fall of the Roman Empire, the Colosseum's purpose shifted drastically. By the 6th century, it was no longer used for grand spectacles and gradually fell into disrepair. The structure was severely damaged by a series of earthquakes, notably in 847 and 1231, which caused significant portions of the southern side to collapse.

During the middle Ages, the Colosseum was repurposed in various ways, including as a fortress by the Frangipane family. By the 12th century, it was largely abandoned and became a quarry for building materials. Its stone was used to construct numerous buildings across Rome, including St. Peter's Basilica, which accelerated its deterioration. Additionally, the metal clamps holding the stones together were stripped away, further weakening the structure.

Efforts to preserve the Colosseum began in earnest during the Renaissance. In 1749, Pope Benedict XIV consecrated the site, declaring it a sacred place due to the early Christian martyrs believed to have died there, although this belief has been largely debunked. This declaration halted further degradation, as it prevented the removal of additional stones.

The modern era of preservation began in the 19th century with extensive restorations initiated under Pope Pius VII. The southern outer wall, which had suffered the most damage, was reinforced to prevent further collapse. Throughout the 20th and 21st centuries, preservation efforts have continued with more sophisticated techniques, including the stabilization of the structure and the cleaning of its surfaces from pollutants.

Preservationists face significant challenges in maintaining the Colosseum. Environmental factors, particularly pollution and the effects of tourism, have been major concerns. The vibrations from nearby traffic and millions of visitors annually contribute to the gradual weakening of the structure. Additionally, the sheer age of the Colosseum means that maintaining its integrity while preserving its historical authenticity is an ongoing struggle.

Today, the Colosseum stands as a testament to both the glory of ancient Rome and the tireless efforts of those committed to its preservation. Despite the challenges, it continues to be one of the most iconic and well-preserved monuments of the ancient world, attracting millions of visitors each year who come to marvel at its enduring majesty.

CHAPTER 7: NEARBY ATTRACTIONS & ACTIVITIES

The Roman Forum

The Roman Forum, or *Forum Romanum*, stands as a testament to the grandeur and complexity of ancient Roman civilization. Once the bustling heart of Rome, the Forum was the epicenter of political, religious, and social activity for centuries. Its ruins today offer visitors a unique glimpse into the daily life and governance of one of history's greatest empires.

Significance of the Roman Forum

The Roman Forum was more than just a marketplace; it was the nucleus of public life in ancient Rome. It housed important government buildings, temples, and monuments that played pivotal roles in the city's administration and religious practices. Key structures like the Senate House (Curia), the Temple of Saturn, and the Arch of Titus illustrate the Forum's importance as a center of power, law, and religious worship.

The Forum's influence extended beyond Rome itself, serving as a model for public spaces in cities throughout the Roman Empire. It was here that Julius Caesar and Augustus, among other notable figures, walked, made decisions, and addressed the people. As such, the Roman Forum is not just a collection of ruins; it is a place where the echoes of history can still be felt.

What to Expect When Exploring the Roman Forum

Visitors to the Roman Forum can expect to traverse a landscape rich in history, where every corner reveals stories of ancient Rome's past. The site is a sprawling complex of ruins, including temples, basilicas, and triumphal arches, each with its own historical significance. As you walk along the ancient cobblestone roads, you can imagine the grandeur of the buildings that once stood there and the bustling life that filled the streets.

Highlights include the Temple of Vesta, where the Vestal Virgins kept the sacred fire burning, and the Arch of Septimius Severus, a triumphal arch celebrating Roman victories. The Forum also offers panoramic views of the surrounding hills, including the Palatine and Capitoline Hills, further enriching the visitor's experience.

Complementing a Visit to the Colosseum

A visit to the Roman Forum perfectly complements a tour of the Colosseum. While the Colosseum showcases the grandeur of Roman engineering and entertainment, the Forum provides insight into the daily workings of Roman society and governance. Together, these sites offer a comprehensive understanding of ancient Rome, from the spectacles of the Colosseum to the political and religious life centered in the Forum.

Palatine Hill

Palatine Hill, one of the most ancient parts of Rome, is a must-visit for history enthusiasts and anyone captivated by the grandeur of the Roman Empire. As the legendary birthplace of Rome, it holds immense historical significance, being the place where Romulus is said to have founded the city in 753 B.C. Over time, Palatine Hill became the favored residence of emperors, aristocrats, and the political elite, making it the epicenter of Roman power and culture.

Historical Importance

Palatine Hill is central to Rome's mythology and history. According to legend, it was here that the she-wolf Lupa nurtured Romulus and Remus, the twin brothers who would eventually play a pivotal role in the founding of Rome. As the city grew, Palatine Hill evolved into the preferred residential area for Rome's most powerful families, including the emperors Augustus, Tiberius, and Domitian, who built opulent palaces on the hill. These palaces were not only luxurious residences but also symbols of imperial authority, making Palatine Hill a symbol of Rome's might.

Key Sites and Views

Visitors to Palatine Hill can explore a rich array of ancient ruins, each offering a glimpse into Rome's illustrious past. One of the most notable sites is the **Domus Augustana**, the palace of Emperor Domitian. This vast complex was designed to impress, with its grand halls, private quarters, and intricate gardens. Nearby, the **House of Augustus** provides a more intimate look at the life of Rome's first emperor, featuring beautifully preserved frescoes and a layout that reflects both grandeur and simplicity.

Another essential stop is the **House of Livia**, the home of Augustus's wife. This residence is famed for its elegant wall paintings, which depict mythological scenes and nature, offering insights into the artistic tastes of the Roman elite.

The **Stadium of Domitian**, a large open space within the palace complex, is another highlight. Though its exact purpose remains debated, it's believed to have been used for private athletic contests or as a garden area.

For breathtaking views, visitors should not miss the **Palatine Museum** and the surrounding terraces. The museum houses artifacts unearthed from the hill, including sculptures, inscriptions, and everyday items that paint a picture of life in ancient Rome. From the terraces, the sweeping views of the Roman Forum and the Circus Maximus provide a striking contrast between the ancient world and the modern city.

Arch of Constantine

The Arch of Constantine, an iconic monument situated between the Colosseum and the Palatine Hill, is one of Rome's most celebrated triumphal arches. Erected in 315 AD, the arch commemorates Emperor Constantine the Great's victory over Maxentius at the Battle of the Milvian Bridge in 312 AD, a pivotal moment that marked the beginning of Constantine's reign and the eventual establishment of Christianity as the dominant religion in the Roman Empire.

This 21-meter-high, 25.9-meter-wide arch stands as a testament to Constantine's power and the political and religious transformation of the Roman Empire. The arch's design is a blend of classical and late antiquity styles, utilizing spolia—reused sculptures and reliefs from earlier monuments, such as those of Emperor Trajan, Hadrian, and Marcus Aurelius. This practice of reappropriation not only emphasized Constantine's connection to these esteemed predecessors but also served as a practical means of construction during a period when resources were scarce.

The iconography of the Arch of Constantine is rich with symbolism. The reliefs depict scenes of Constantine's military prowess, divine favor, and generosity, aligning him with Rome's historical legacy of great emperors. Notably, the arch features a frieze that narrates the story of Constantine's victory, his entry into Rome, and his clemency towards his vanquished foes. The use of Christian symbols, like the Chi-Rho (a Christian monogram) on the shields of Constantine's soldiers, subtly marks the shift from Rome's pagan past to its Christian future, reflecting Constantine's role as the first Roman emperor to convert to Christianity.

The Arch of Constantine's proximity to the Colosseum is significant both geographically and symbolically. It stands as a bridge between the old and the new, connecting the glory of Rome's imperial past, as embodied by the Colosseum, with the emerging Christian era initiated by Constantine. The Colosseum, a symbol of Roman engineering and entertainment, contrasts with the Arch's emphasis on military triumph and divine providence. Together, they encapsulate the dual narrative of Rome: one of conquest and spectacle, the other of transformation and the embrace of a new spiritual order.

For visitors to the Colosseum, the Arch of Constantine provides a poignant reminder of Rome's complex history, where the past and future converge in stone and symbolism. It invites contemplation on the evolution of Roman power, from the grandeur of the gladiatorial games to the dawn of a Christian empire.

Capitoline Museums

The Capitoline Museums, located on Rome's Capitoline Hill, are among the oldest public museums in the world, offering a deep dive into the rich history of ancient Rome. Established in 1471 when Pope Sixtus IV donated a collection of bronze statues to the people of Rome, the museums have grown to house an extensive array of artifacts that provide invaluable insights into Rome's imperial past, including exhibits that enhance the understanding of the Colosseum and its era.

Overview of the Museums

The Capitoline Museums are spread across two main buildings: the Palazzo dei Conservatori and the Palazzo Nuovo, connected by an underground gallery that also houses the Tabularium, an ancient Roman archive. These museums feature a vast collection of Roman art, sculpture, and archaeological finds, making them an essential stop for anyone looking to understand the grandeur and complexity of ancient Rome.

Exhibits Relevant to the Colosseum

1. **The Colossus of Constantine**: One of the most striking exhibits relevant to the Colosseum is the Colossus of Constantine. Originally, part of a massive statue that stood in the Basilica of Maxentius, its remnants, including a giant head and hand, are displayed in the Palazzo dei Conservatori. This statue represents the type of imperial propaganda and grandeur that characterized the Colosseum's era, offering insights into the political and cultural context in which the Colosseum operated.

2. **The Dying Gaul**: This iconic sculpture, housed in the Palazzo Nuovo, depicts a defeated Gallic warrior in his final moments. The statue is a poignant reminder of the brutal realities of war, a theme that resonates with the gladiatorial combats of the Colosseum. It exemplifies the Roman celebration of victory and the valorization of defeated foes, mirroring the narratives often depicted in the arena.

3. **Roman Portraiture**: The extensive collection of Roman busts and statues in the Capitoline Museums provides a detailed look at the individuals, who shaped Roman history, including emperors, senators, and gladiators. Understanding these figures enhances the visitor's comprehension of the Colosseum, as it was these very people who frequented and defined its social and political significance.

4. **The Capitoline Wolf**: Though not directly linked to the Colosseum, the Capitoline Wolf, a bronze statue depicting the she-wolf suckling Romulus and Remus, symbolizes the founding myth of Rome.

This exhibit connects visitors to the origins of Roman civilization, contextualizing the Colosseum as a product of the city's legendary and storied past. A visit to the Capitoline Museums is not only a journey through ancient Rome but also a complementary experience to exploring the Colosseum. The artifacts and exhibits provide a deeper understanding of the social, political, and cultural milieu of the era, enriching the visitor's appreciation of Rome's most iconic monument.

Piazza Venezia & Vittorio Emanuele II Monument

Piazza Venezia, often considered the heart of Rome, is a bustling square steeped in historical and cultural significance. Serving as a central hub for many of the city's major roads, it offers a gateway to some of Rome's most iconic landmarks, including the Colosseum, the Roman Forum, and Via del Corso, one of the city's main shopping streets.

At the center of Piazza Venezia stands the towering Vittorio Emanuele II Monument, also known as the "Altare della Patria" (Altar of the Fatherland). This grandiose structure was built in honor of Vittorio Emanuele II, the first king of a unified Italy, and is a symbol of Italian unification and nationalism. Constructed between 1885 and 1925, the monument is made of white marble and features a massive equestrian statue of Vittorio Emanuele II at its core. The monument's design includes a series of grand staircases, towering columns, and allegorical statues representing various Italian regions and virtues like unity, liberty, and law.

The Vittorio Emanuele II Monument also houses the Tomb of the Unknown Soldier, a solemn site dedicated to Italy's fallen soldiers. Guarded by an eternal flame and military sentinels, it is a place of national pride and reflection, especially on important days like Republic Day (June 2nd) and Armistice Day (November 4th).

Visitors can explore the monument by ascending to the upper terraces, which offer breathtaking panoramic views of Rome's historic center. From here, you can see the Colosseum, the Roman Forum, the Palatine Hill, and even St. Peter's Basilica in the distance. These views alone make it a worthwhile stop for anyone exploring the area.

Incorporating Piazza Venezia and the Vittorio Emanuele II Monument into your itinerary is easy and rewarding. The piazza is a convenient starting or ending point for a day of sightseeing in Rome. Given its proximity to the Colosseum and the Roman Forum, it is ideal to visit the monument either before or after exploring these ancient sites. The area is also well connected by public transportation, making it accessible from other parts of the city.

Whether you are a history enthusiast or simply looking to experience the grandeur of Rome, a visit to Piazza Venezia and the Vittorio Emanuele II Monument provides a deeper understanding of Italy's rich heritage and offers a unique perspective on the Eternal City.

CHAPTER 8: CULTURAL TIPS

Italian Etiquette & Customs

Greetings and Social Interactions

Italians are known for their warmth and friendliness. A common greeting involves a handshake, accompanied by a smile and direct eye contact. Among friends and family, it's customary to exchange two light kisses on the cheeks, starting with the right. Always use formal titles like "Signore" (Mr.) or "Signora" (Mrs.) when addressing someone, especially in professional or formal settings, until you are invited to use their first name.

Dining Etiquette

Mealtime is a cherished social occasion in Italy, and there are several customs to keep in mind. Always wait for the host to begin the meal before starting to eat. It is polite to eat slowly and enjoy the food, as meals are seen as an opportunity for conversation and enjoyment. When dining at a restaurant, tipping is not obligatory but leaving a small amount, typically around 5-10% of the bill is appreciated for exceptional service. Avoid asking for substitutions or modifications to dishes, as Italian chefs take great pride in their culinary creations.

Dress Code

Italians value style and appearance, and dressing well is a sign of respect. When visiting churches or religious sites, ensure your shoulders and knees are covered as a mark of respect. In general, opting for smart-casual attire rather than overly casual clothing will help you blend in and show respect for local customs.

Punctuality and Appointments

While Italians are generally relaxed about time, punctuality is appreciated in business settings. For social events, it is common to arrive a little late—about 15 minutes after the scheduled time is considered polite. If you are meeting someone for the first time, bringing a small gift, such as a bottle of wine or flowers, is a thoughtful gesture.

Public Behavior

Italians are expressive and often engage in animated conversations, but it's important to remain polite and avoid raising your voice in public settings. When visiting museums or historic sites like the Colosseum, speak quietly and avoid disrupting others. It is also customary to say

"Buongiorno" (Good morning) or "Buonasera" (Good evening) when entering shops, restaurants, or public places.

Respect for History and Tradition

Italy's rich history is a source of pride, and visitors should show respect when visiting historical sites. Follow all posted rules, such as not touching artifacts or taking flash photography, and always dispose of litter properly.

Tipping Guidelines

Restaurants and Cafes

In most restaurants and cafes, a service charge (called "coperto") is often included in the bill. This charge usually covers bread, table settings, and basic service. Therefore, leaving an additional tip is not obligatory but can be a nice gesture if the service was particularly good. A tip of 5-10% of the total bill is generous and will be appreciated by the staff. In more casual settings, like cafes or trattorias, rounding up the bill to the nearest euro or leaving a few coins is perfectly acceptable.

Guided Tours

For guided tours of the Colosseum, tipping your guide is customary, especially if they provided an informative and enjoyable experience. A typical tip would range from €5 to €10 per person, depending on the length and quality of the tour. If you are part of a larger group, consider giving a higher tip to recognize the guide's effort in managing the group and ensuring everyone had a good experience.

Taxis and Transportation

Tipping taxi drivers in Italy is not expected, but rounding up to, the nearest euro is common practice. For example, if your fare is €18, you might round up to €20. If the driver assists with luggage or provides an exceptionally pleasant ride, adding an extra euro or two as a token of appreciation is a kind gesture. For private car, services or transfers arranged in advance, a tip of €5 to €10 is generally appropriate, depending on the distance traveled and the service provided.

Hotel Staff

In hotels near the Colosseum, tipping is not mandatory but is appreciated for certain services. For bellhops or porters who assist with your luggage, a tip of €1 to €2 per bag is standard. Housekeeping staff can be tipped €1 to €2 per day, left in the room with a note indicating that it is for them. If a concierge goes out of their way to help you with reservations or special requests, a tip of €5 to €10 is a considerate gesture.

Other Services

For other services, such as hairdressers or spa treatments, it is common to leave a small tip of around 5-10% of the service cost. Again, tipping is not obligatory, but it is appreciated for excellent service.

How to Behave Respectfully at Historical Sites

1. Follow the Rules and Regulations

Every historical site has specific rules in place to protect its integrity. At the Colosseum, you will find signs indicating where you can and cannot go, as well as rules against touching the structures, climbing on ruins, or entering restricted areas. Always adhere to these regulations—they are designed to preserve the site for future generations.

2. Keep Noise Levels Down

The Colosseum, like many historical sites, is a place for reflection and learning. Avoid loud conversations, shouting, or playing music. Remember that many visitors come to these sites for a contemplative experience, so keeping noise to a minimum helps maintain a respectful atmosphere.

3. Avoid Littering and Vandalism

Littering is not only disrespectful but also harmful to these ancient sites. Always dispose of your trash in designated bins, and if you see litter, consider picking it up to help keep the area clean. Vandalism, such as carving your name into walls or defacing property, is a criminal act and severely damages these irreplaceable historical treasures. Never engage in or tolerate such behaviour.

4. Respect the Environment

The areas surrounding the Colosseum and other historical sites often include gardens, parks, or archaeological remains. Avoid trampling on plants, disturbing wildlife, or removing any objects, including stones or fragments, as souvenirs. These are part of the site's heritage and should remain in place.

5. Photography Etiquette

While photography is generally allowed at the Colosseum, be mindful of how you use your camera. Avoid using flash in areas where it is prohibited, as it can damage ancient frescoes and artifacts. When taking photos, be considerate of other visitors by not blocking pathways or obstructing views.

6. Be Mindful of Cultural Sensitivities

The Colosseum is a place of historical and cultural significance, and in some cases, it may also be a site of remembrance. Be respectful by dressing appropriately—avoiding overly casual or revealing attire—and by refraining from behaviour that could be seen as disrespectful, such as inappropriate gestures or posing in a manner that trivializes the site's history.

7. Avoid Disrupting Tours and Other Visitors

If you are part of a guided tour, listen attentively and avoid interrupting the guide. If you are exploring on your own, give space to tour groups and other visitors. Everyone deserves a chance to experience the site without disruptions.

CHAPTER 9: ACCOMMODATIONS

Best Neighborhoods to Stay Near the Colosseum

Monti

Monti is often hailed as one of the most charming neighborhoods in Rome and is just a short walk from the Colosseum. This historic district boasts cobblestone streets, ancient churches, and a vibrant atmosphere that blends old-world charm with a modern edge. Monti is ideal for visitors who appreciate boutique shopping, cozy cafes, and authentic Roman trattorias. Staying in Monti means you can explore the Colosseum in the morning and return in the evening to enjoy the lively local nightlife. The neighborhood's proximity to the metro station also makes it easy to explore other parts of Rome.

Celio

Celio is another excellent option, offering a quieter, more residential feel while still being incredibly close to the Colosseum. This area is perfect for those who prefer a more laid-back environment with green spaces like the Parco di Colle Oppio, which offers stunning views of the Colosseum. Celio is also home to several important churches, including the Basilica of San Clemente, making it a great spot for history enthusiasts. The neighborhood is well-connected by bus routes, and its quieter streets offer a more relaxed stay while keeping you within walking distance of the major attractions.

Esquilino

Esquilino, located just north of the Colosseum, is a culturally diverse neighborhood known for its bustling markets and eclectic dining scene. This area is particularly convenient for visitors who arrive by train, as it is close to

Termini Station, Rome's main transportation hub. Esquilino offers a wide range of accommodation options, from budget-friendly hotels to more upscale choices. The neighborhood's central location makes it easy to reach not only the Colosseum but also other iconic sites like the Roman Forum and the Basilica di Santa Maria Maggiore. It's a lively area that offers a mix of traditional Roman culture and multicultural influences.

Aventine Hill

For those seeking a more tranquil setting, Aventine Hill is a lesser known. While it's slightly further from the Colosseum compared to Monti or Celio, it offers breathtaking views of Rome and a peaceful atmosphere. Aventine Hill is known for its beautiful gardens, historic churches, and the famous Keyhole of Rome. Staying here provides a serene retreat after a day of sightseeing, with the Colosseum just a short bus or taxi ride away. It's ideal for travelers who want to combine the convenience of proximity to major attractions with the serenity of a quieter neighborhood.

Luxury Hotels

Palazzo Manfredi - A Relais & Châteaux Hotel

- **Address**: Via Labicana, 125, 00184 Rome, Italy
- **Price**: Starting from €800 per night
- **Amenities**: Palazzo Manfredi is an opulent boutique hotel that offers stunning views of the Colosseum from many of its rooms. Guests can enjoy personalized services, including private transfers and concierge services. The hotel features a rooftop terrace, perfect for dining with a panoramic view of the Colosseum. Additional amenities include free Wi-Fi, a fitness center, and in-room spa services. The rooms are elegantly furnished with luxurious linens, marble bathrooms, and modern entertainment systems.

Hotel Palazzo Manfredi – Relais & Châteaux

- **Address**: Via Labicana, 125, 00184 Rome, Italy
- **Price**: Starting from €1,200 per night
- **Amenities**: With a prime location overlooking the Colosseum, Hotel Palazzo Manfredi offers an exclusive and intimate experience. The hotel boasts a Michelin-starred restaurant, AROMA, which

serves gourmet Italian cuisine with a view. Guests can indulge in the hotel's well-appointed rooms, featuring king-sized beds, marble bathrooms, and high-end toiletries. The hotel also provides a complimentary breakfast, 24-hour room service, and a rooftop lounge bar.

Hotel Capo d'Africa – Colosseo

- **Address**: Via Capo d'Africa, 54, 00184 Rome, Italy
- **Price**: Starting from €350 per night
- **Amenities**: Located just a short walk from the Colosseum, Hotel Capo d'Africa combines contemporary style with historical elements. The hotel features spacious rooms with modern décor, a rooftop terrace offering breathtaking views, and an on-site gym. Guests can enjoy a delicious breakfast buffet on the terrace and have access to concierge services, free Wi-Fi, and meeting rooms. The hotel also offers bike rentals for those wishing to explore Rome on two wheels.

The Inn at the Roman Forum

- **Address**: Via degli Ibernesi, 30, 00184 Rome, Italy
- **Price**: Starting from €500 per night

- **Amenities**: A lesser known within walking distance of the Colosseum, The Inn at the Roman Forum offers a unique experience with its blend of ancient and modern design. The hotel features an archaeological site within its premises, giving guests a rare glimpse into Rome's past. Rooms are luxuriously appointed with rich fabrics, marble bathrooms, and high-end amenities. The hotel provides a complimentary breakfast, a rooftop terrace, and a 24-hour concierge service.

Budget-Friendly Options

The Beehive

- **Address**: Via Marghera, 8, 00185 Rome, Italy
- **Price per Night**: From €50
- **Overview**: A cozy, eco-friendly hostel located just a 20-minute walk from the Colosseum, The Beehive is a favorite among budget travelers. It offers both private rooms and dormitory-style accommodations. Guests can enjoy a communal kitchen, a peaceful garden, and regular social events, making it easy to meet fellow travelers.

Hotel Centro Cavour

- **Address**: Via Cavour, 233, 00184 Rome, Italy
- **Price per Night**: From €60
- **Overview**: Just a 10-minute walk from the Colosseum, Hotel Centro Cavour is a great option for travelers seeking comfort on a budget. The rooms are simple yet comfortable, with modern amenities like free Wi-Fi and air conditioning. The hotel is also close to the Cavour metro station, making it easy to explore other parts of Rome.

Generator Rome

- **Address**: Via Principe Amedeo, 251, 00185 Rome, Italy
- **Price per Night**: From €40
- **Overview**: Part of the popular Generator chain, this stylish hostel is located in Rome's Esquilino district, a short walk from the Colosseum. The hostel offers a mix of dormitory beds and private rooms, along with trendy common areas, a bar, and a café. It's perfect for younger travelers who want a lively atmosphere without breaking the bank.

Casa San Giuseppe

- **Address**: Lungotevere De' Cenci, 00186 Rome, Italy
- **Price per Night**: From €65
- **Overview**: Located in the historic Trastevere neighborhood, Casa San Giuseppe offers a peaceful retreat within walking distance of the Colosseum. The rooms are clean and well-maintained, and the hotel provides a complimentary breakfast. The tranquil setting makes it ideal for those who want a quiet, budget-friendly stay.

B&B Second Floor

- **Address**: Via San Giovanni in Laterano, 10, 00184 Rome, Italy
- **Price per Night**: From €55
- **Overview**: This charming bed and breakfast is situated right next to the Colosseum. The rooms are bright and modern, and some even offer views of the ancient amphitheater. With its prime location and reasonable rates, B&B Second Floor offers exceptional value for money.

Tips for Saving Money

- **Book Early**: Rome is a popular destination, and booking your accommodation several months in advance can help you secure lower rates.
- **Travel Off-Peak**: Visiting during the shoulder seasons (spring or fall) often results in lower accommodation prices and fewer crowds.
- **Use Public Transport**: Staying slightly further from the Colosseum can reduce costs significantly. The city's public transport system is efficient and affordable, allowing you to explore Rome without overspending.

Hostels & Boutique Stays

The Yellow Hostel

- **Address**: Via Palestro, 44, 00185 Rome, Italy
- **Price per Night**: Starting at €25 for a dorm bed, €80 for a private room.

The Yellow Hostel is a favorite among young travelers looking for a lively social scene. Located just a short metro ride from the Colosseum, this hostel is renowned for its vibrant atmosphere, complete with live music, rooftop parties, and organized social events. The on-site bar and restaurant, which offers discounted meals for guests, adds to the appeal. The hostel's modern amenities, including free Wi-Fi, a communal kitchen, and a travel desk, ensure a comfortable stay for budget-conscious travelers.

Generator Rome

- **Address**: Via Principe Amedeo, 257, 00185 Rome, Italy
- **Price per Night**: Dorm beds from €35, private rooms from €120.

Generator Rome combines stylish design with a central location, making it an excellent choice for those who want to be close to the action. This boutique hostel features a chic interior with contemporary art, comfortable lounge areas, and a rooftop terrace offering stunning views of the city. The Colosseum is easily accessible by foot or metro. Guests can enjoy the hostel's bar, which serves up local wines and cocktails, as well as an in-house café offering Italian pastries and coffee.

The Beehive

- **Address**: Via Marghera, 8, 00185 Rome, Italy
- **Price per Night**: Private rooms from €90, dorm beds from €40.

The Beehive is a charming boutique hostel that combines the comfort of a hotel with the community vibe of a hostel. Located near Termini Station, it offers easy access to the Colosseum and other major attractions. The Beehive prides itself on sustainability, with eco-friendly practices and a focus on organic, locally sourced ingredients in its on-site café. The cozy garden courtyard is perfect for relaxing after a day of exploring, and the hostel regularly hosts yoga classes and communal dinners, fostering a sense of community among guests.

Nerva Boutique Hotel

- **Address**: Via Tor de' Conti, 3/4, 00184 Rome, Italy
- **Price per Night**: Starting at €150.

Located just steps away from the Colosseum and the Roman Forum, Nerva Boutique Hotel offers a luxurious yet intimate stay. Each room is uniquely decorated with a mix of modern and vintage furnishings, creating a cozy and elegant atmosphere. Guests are treated to a complimentary breakfast each morning, featuring freshly baked pastries and local specialties. The hotel's personalized service and prime location make it an ideal choice for travelers looking for a more private, upscale experience without the price tag of a larger hotel.

CHAPTER 10: DINING & SHOPPING

Restaurants with a View of the Colosseum

Aroma Restaurant

Located on the rooftop of the Palazzo Manfredi hotel, Aroma is a Michelin-starred restaurant that offers an unparalleled view of the Colosseum. The intimate setting, with its panoramic terrace, makes it a perfect spot for a romantic dinner or a special occasion. Chef Giuseppe Di Iorio crafts contemporary Italian dishes with a focus on quality ingredients and elegant presentation. A must-try dish is the "Spaghettoni with Sea Urchin," which perfectly balances the rich flavors of the sea with delicate pasta. The "Lamb Chops with Roman Artichokes" is another highlight, offering a modern twist on traditional Roman flavors.

Ristorante Roof Garden

Perched atop the Hotel Forum, Ristorante Roof Garden offers a breathtaking view of not only the Colosseum but also the Roman Forum and Palatine Hill. The restaurant's ambiance is elegant yet relaxed, making it ideal for both lunch and dinner. The menu features a mix of classic Roman dishes and Mediterranean cuisine. Start with the "Supplì al Telefono," a Roman rice ball stuffed with mozzarella, followed by the "Saltimbocca alla Romana," a traditional Roman dish of veal, prosciutto, and sage, cooked to perfection. The "Tiramisù" here is a delightful way to end your meal while gazing at the illuminated Colosseum.

La Terrazza del Cesari

Situated on the rooftop of the Hotel Cesari, La Terrazza del Cesari offers a cozy and more informal dining experience with a stunning view of the Colosseum in the distance. Known for its friendly service and relaxed atmosphere, this restaurant is perfect for a casual meal. The menu features a variety of Roman classics, with a particular emphasis on pasta dishes. Try the "Cacio e Pepe," a simple yet flavorful dish of pasta tossed with pecorino cheese and black pepper, or the "Gnocchi alla Sorrentina," soft potato gnocchi baked with tomato sauce and mozzarella. Pair your meal with a glass of local wine for the full Roman experience.

Oppio Caffè

For a more laid-back option, Oppio Caffè offers casual dining with a direct view of the Colosseum. Located on via delle Terme di Tito, this café is ideal for a quick bite or a relaxing drink after exploring the Colosseum. The menu includes a variety of sandwiches, salads, and pizzas, but the "Margherita Pizza" is a standout, offering a taste of Italy's culinary heritage in a setting that is hard to beat.

Traditional Roman Cuisine to Try

1. Cacio e Pepe

A quintessential Roman pasta dish, Cacio e Pepe is as simple as it is delicious. Made with just Pecorino Romano cheese, black pepper, and pasta, this dish is a perfect example of Roman culinary restraint and skill. For an authentic experience, head to **Flavio al Velavevodetto** in the Testaccio district, a short taxi ride from the Colosseum, known for perfecting this classic.

2. *Carbonara*

Rome's most famous pasta dish, Carbonara, is a creamy, savory delight made with eggs, Pecorino Romano cheese, guanciale (cured pork cheek), and black pepper. The secret lies in the creamy sauce, which is made without cream but achieves its texture through expertly timed cooking. **Trattoria Da Enzo al 29** in Trastevere is revered for its traditional take on Carbonara, making it worth the short journey from the Colosseum.

3. *Amatriciana*

Originating from the nearby town of Amatrice, this tomato-based pasta sauce features guanciale and Pecorino Romano cheese, offering a slightly spicy kick from chili peppers. The dish is most commonly served with bucatini or spaghetti. For a taste of authentic Amatriciana, **Hostaria Romana**, located just a 10-minute walk from the Colosseum, is a top choice.

4. *Saltimbocca alla Romana*

A classic Roman secondi (main course), Saltimbocca alla Romana consists of thin veal slices topped with prosciutto and sage, cooked in white wine and butter. The flavors are rich and comforting. For an excellent version, try **Ristorante La Taverna dei Fori Imperiali**, which is located close to the Roman Forum and offers a traditional dining experience.

5. *Carciofi alla Romana*

Artichokes are a staple of Roman cuisine, and Carciofi alla Romana (Roman-style artichokes) is a beloved preparation. The artichokes are stuffed with garlic, mint, and parsley, then slowly braised in olive oil and white wine until tender. To taste this dish at its best, visit **Da Giggetto**, located in the Jewish Ghetto, a historic neighborhood within walking distance of the Colosseum.

6. *Supplì*

These fried rice balls, filled with mozzarella, are the Roman answer to arancini. Crunchy on the outside and gooey on the inside, they make for a perfect snack or appetizer. For the best Supplì, stop by **I Supplì** in Trastevere, a bit further from the Colosseum but worth the detour for their crispy, flavorful treats.

Best Cafes & Gelato Spots Nearby

Antico Caffè Santamaria

- **Address**: Piazza di S. Maria Maggiore, 1, 00185 Rome, Italy
- **Phone**: +39 06 488 2651
- **What Makes It Special**: Located just a short walk from the Colosseum, Antico Caffè Santamaria is a local favorite known for its rich espresso and classic Italian pastries. The cozy atmosphere and prime location make it an ideal stop to enjoy a cappuccino while soaking in the Roman vibe. The outdoor seating area provides a pleasant setting to watch the city's life unfold.

La Bottega del Caffè

- **Address**: Piazza Madonna dei Monti, 5, 00184 Rome, Italy
- **Phone**: +39 06 488 0422
- **What Makes It Special**: Nestled in the charming Monti neighborhood, this café offers a blend of history and modernity. La Bottega del Caffè is

popular for its expertly brewed coffee and its laid-back, artsy vibe. The café's location in a quaint piazza adds to its appeal, making it a perfect spot for people-watching. Don't miss their selection of fresh pastries and light bites.

Gelateria La Dolce Vita

- **Address**: Via Cavour, 306, 00184 Rome, Italy
- **Phone**: +39 06 4891 3157
- **What Makes It Special**: A stone's throw from the Colosseum, Gelateria La Dolce Vita is a must-visit for gelato lovers. Known for its all-natural ingredients and wide range of flavors, this gelateria offers everything from traditional choices like pistachio and stracciatella to more adventurous options. The creamy texture and authentic taste make it a standout.

Fassi Gelateria

- **Address**: Via Principe Eugenio, 65, 00185 Rome, Italy
- **Phone**: +39 06 446 4740
- **What Makes It Special**: Established in 1880, Fassi Gelateria is one of Rome's oldest and most beloved

gelato shops. Often referred to as the "Palazzo del Freddo" (Palace of the Cold), it offers an extensive selection of flavors, all made with high-quality ingredients. The historic ambiance adds a unique charm, making it more than just a stop for gelato but an experience in itself.

Ciuri Ciuri

- **Address**: Via Leonina, 18, 00184 Rome, Italy
- **Phone**: +39 06 482 6660
- **What Makes It Special**: Specializing in Sicilian pastries and gelato, Ciuri Ciuri brings a taste of Sicily to the heart of Rome. Their cannoli are particularly famous, pairing perfectly with a scoop of their rich gelato. The vibrant interior and friendly service make it a delightful spot for a sweet break.

Souvenir Shops and Local Artisans

1. Mercato Monti Urban Market

Located just a short walk from the Colosseum, Mercato Monti is a must-visit for travelers seeking unique, handmade souvenirs. This eclectic market is a hub for local artisans and designers, offering everything from vintage clothing and handmade jewelry to art prints and leather goods. The items here are often one-of-a-kind, making it a perfect spot to find a truly special memento of your trip.

2. Bottega del Marmoraro

For something truly Roman, head to Bottega del Marmoraro, a small workshop near the Colosseum that specializes in marble carvings. Here, you can purchase intricately carved marble plaques, often engraved with Latin phrases or symbols of ancient Rome. The artisan behind the counter can even customize a piece for you, adding a personal touch to your souvenir.

3. Cereria Di Giorgio

This historic candle shop, established in 1880, is located in the heart of Rome and offers beautifully crafted candles that make for elegant souvenirs. Cereria Di Giorgio is renowned for its high-quality wax and traditional methods. You can find candles shaped like Roman columns or with intricate designs inspired by ancient Roman art. These candles not only serve as beautiful decorations but also as reminders of the city is enduring artisanship.

4. Via Sannio Market

If you prefer a more traditional market experience, visit Via Sannio Market, a bustling flea market where you can find a wide array of goods. Among the vintage clothing and accessories, you'll discover locally crafted jewelry, hand-painted ceramics, and other artisanal products. Haggling is part of the experience here, so be prepared to negotiate for a good deal on a unique piece.

5. Campo de' Fiori

Although known primarily as a food market, Campo de' Fiori also features stalls with local crafts. Early in the morning, you can find artisans selling hand-painted ceramics, leather goods, and embroidered textiles. These items make for practical and beautiful souvenirs that showcase the skills of local craftspeople.

6. Eataly Rome

For a culinary souvenir, visit Eataly Rome, where you can purchase high-quality Italian food products. From extra virgin olive oil to artisanal pasta and locally produced wine, these items bring the flavors of Rome back home with you. Many of the products are made by small, family-owned businesses, ensuring that your purchase supports local producers.

CHAPTER 11: DAY TRIPS FROM ROME

Pompeii & Mount Vesuvius

Travel Time and Logistics

The trip begins with an early morning departure from Rome. Most visitors opt for the high-speed train to Naples, which takes around 1 to 1.5 hours. From Naples, it's a quick 30-minute local train ride on the Circumvesuviana line to Pompeii. Alternatively, guided tours often include direct transportation, making logistics simpler and more convenient.

Exploring Pompeii

Upon arrival in Pompeii, visitors are greeted by the remarkably preserved ruins of a once-thriving Roman city, buried under volcanic ash and pumice after the catastrophic eruption of Mount Vesuvius in 79 AD. The site spans 170 acres, with many areas still being excavated, but there is plenty to see in a day.

Highlights of Pompeii include the Forum, where the city's political, religious, and commercial activities took place. Nearby, the haunting casts of Pompeii's residents, immortalized in their final moments, serve as a poignant reminder of the eruption's devastating impact. The Amphitheatre, one of the oldest surviving Roman arenas, and the House of the Faun, known for its intricate mosaics, are also must-see sites.

As you wander through the ancient streets, you'll encounter well-preserved homes, baths, and shops, offering a glimpse into daily life in a bustling Roman city. Audio guides and maps are available to help navigate the site, but hiring a local guide can provide deeper insights and enrich your experience.

Ascending Mount Vesuvius

After exploring Pompeii, many travelers continue to Mount Vesuvius, just a short bus or taxi ride away. The ascent to the volcano's summit involves a moderately challenging hike of about 30 minutes from the parking area. The effort is rewarded with panoramic views of the Bay of Naples and the surrounding landscape, along with the awe-inspiring sight of the crater itself.

Standing at the edge of the crater, it's hard not to feel a sense of awe, knowing this dormant giant once unleashed such destructive power. On a clear day, the views from the summit are breathtaking, offering a striking contrast between the tranquil scenery and the volcano's turbulent past.

Tivoli: Villa d'Este & Hadrian's Villa

Villa d'Este: Renaissance Elegance

Villa d'Este is a masterpiece of Renaissance architecture and garden design, renowned for its terraced hillside gardens, intricate fountains, and lush greenery. As you wander through the villa, you are transported to a world of opulence and elegance, reflecting the tastes and aspirations of Cardinal Ippolito II d'Este, who commissioned the villa in the 16th century. The highlight of the visit is undoubtedly the gardens, where water features are ingeniously integrated into the landscape, creating a symphony of cascading water, playful fountains, and serene ponds. The most famous of these is the Fountain of Neptune, which stands as a majestic centerpiece among the terraced levels. The villa itself is adorned with frescoes

134

and art that celebrate the grandeur of the Renaissance, offering a serene contrast to the rugged history of the Colosseum.

Hadrian's Villa: Imperial Grandeur

Just a short drive from Villa d'Este lies Hadrian's Villa, an expansive complex that served as the retreat of Emperor Hadrian during the 2nd century AD. This site is a testament to the architectural and engineering prowess of ancient Rome. Spread over 250 acres, Hadrian's Villa was designed to mimic the most beautiful places in the Roman Empire, incorporating Greek, Egyptian, and Roman architectural elements. Walking through the remains of its palaces, temples, and baths, visitors can imagine the luxury and power that once defined this imperial residence. The Canopus, a long reflecting pool flanked by statues and columns, is particularly striking, offering a glimpse into the opulence that characterized Hadrian's reign.

Complementing the Colosseum

While the Colosseum immerses visitors in the grandeur and spectacle of ancient Rome's public life, a visit to Tivoli's Villa d'Este and Hadrian's Villa provides a more intimate exploration of Rome's cultural and architectural sophistication. Villa d'Este showcases the artistic and aesthetic sensibilities of the Renaissance, while Hadrian's Villa highlights the personal tastes and imperial power of one of Rome's greatest emperors. Together, these sites offer a rounded perspective of Roman history, from the imperial ambitions encapsulated by the Colosseum to the private and contemplative spaces of Tivoli. This combination of experiences deepens the understanding of Rome's legacy, making it a must-see for any traveler seeking to fully appreciate the richness of Italy's past.

Ostia Antica

Ostia Antica, the once-thriving port city of ancient Rome, offers a unique and invaluable perspective on the everyday life of Roman citizens. Unlike the grandeur of the Colosseum, which highlights the entertainment and social spectacles of ancient Rome, Ostia Antica provides insight into the more mundane, yet equally fascinating, aspects of Roman civilization. Located at the mouth of the Tiber

River, Ostia was Rome's primary seaport, serving as a bustling hub for trade and commerce.

Historical Significance of Ostia Antica

Founded in the 4th century BCE, Ostia Antica played a crucial role in the economic and military expansion of Rome. As the city's primary seaport, it was the gateway through which goods, including grain, oil, and wine, flowed into Rome. The strategic location of Ostia made it a vital asset in securing Rome's food supply, especially during the empire's peak. The city's decline began in the 3rd century CE, as the Tiber's course shifted and the port of Portus was constructed nearby. Eventually, the city was abandoned and left to be buried under layers of silt and sediment, preserving its structures remarkably well.

A Different Perspective on Roman Life

Visiting Ostia Antica offers a unique opportunity to explore a well-preserved Roman town that was less about the splendor of the elite and more about the daily lives of ordinary citizens. Unlike the urban density of Rome, Ostia provides a more relaxed environment where visitors can stroll through wide streets, explore residential areas, and see the remains of public baths, taverns, and warehouses.

One of the most striking aspects of Ostia is the preservation of its buildings, including multi-story apartment blocks (insulae), which give a clear picture of how most Romans lived. These insulae, often overlooked in grand narratives of Roman history, highlight the communal lifestyle of Rome's middle and lower classes. The remains of shops, bakeries, and even public latrines provide a vivid snapshot of daily activities and the practicalities of urban life.

The city's mosaics, frescoes, and public buildings, such as the Capitolium and the theater, offer further insights into the social and religious life of its inhabitants. The Mithraeum, dedicated to the god Mithras, is a particularly interesting site, revealing the religious diversity that existed alongside the state-sanctioned Roman pantheon.

Florence & Pisa (Day Trip Options)

Getting There

Start your day early by catching the high-speed train from Rome to Florence. The journey takes about 1.5 hours, making it the quickest and most efficient way to reach Florence. From Florence, Pisa is just an additional hour by train, allowing you to comfortably visit both cities in one day.

Florence: The Cradle of the Renaissance

Begin your day in Florence, the birthplace of the Renaissance, where art and history are on full display. Upon arrival, head straight to the **Piazza del Duomo**, home to Florence's most famous landmark, the **Cathedral of Santa Maria del Fiore** (the Duomo). Admire its stunning facade and, if time permits, climb the 463 steps to the top of the dome for panoramic views of the city.

Next, make your way to the **Uffizi Gallery**, one of the most important art museums in the world. Here, you can marvel at masterpieces by Botticelli, Leonardo da Vinci, and Michelangelo. Given time constraints, consider focusing on the highlights of the collection to ensure you don't miss the most renowned works.

Afterward, stroll to the **Ponte Vecchio**, the medieval stone bridge lined with charming jewelry shops. From there, head to the **Piazza della Signoria**, an open-air museum filled with sculptures, including a replica of Michelangelo's David.

Pisa: The Leaning Tower and Beyond

In the afternoon, take the train to Pisa. The main attraction here is, of course, the **Leaning Tower of Pisa**. Located in the **Piazza dei Miracoli** (Square of Miracles), this architectural wonder is a must-see. Spend some time exploring the square, which also houses the **Pisa Cathedral** and **Baptistery**. If you are up for it, climb the Leaning Tower for a unique perspective of Pisa.

Maximizing Your Time

To make the most of your day, plan your itinerary carefully and book tickets in advance, especially for the Uffizi Gallery and the Leaning Tower, as lines can be long. Consider a guided tour that covers both cities to ensure you hit all the highlights without wasting time navigating on your own. If you prefer independent travel, make sure to account for travel time between attractions and the train schedules.

CHAPTER 12: SAFETY TIPS & EMERGENCY INFORMATION

Staying Safe at the Colosseum

Security Tips

1. **Beware of Pickpockets**: The Colosseum, like many popular tourist attractions, can attract pickpockets. Keep your valuables secure in a money belt or an anti-theft bag. Avoid carrying large amounts of cash, and be cautious when someone bumps into you, as this could be a distraction tactic.

2. **Stay Alert in Crowds**: The Colosseum is often crowded, especially during peak tourist season. Be mindful of your surroundings, particularly in queues and crowded areas. Stay close to your group and keep your belongings within sight at all times.

3. **Use Official Services**: Only purchase tickets from official sources, such as the Colosseum's official website or authorized ticket vendors. Beware of touts selling "skip-the-line" tickets or guided tours outside the entrance, as these may be scams or overpriced.

4. **Follow Security Procedures**: The Colosseum has strict security checks at the entrance, including bag inspections and metal detectors. To speed up the process, bring only essential items, and avoid carrying large bags or backpacks. Note that items such as sharp objects, large umbrellas, and glass bottles are prohibited.

5. **Avoid Unauthorized Vendors**: Throughout the area, you'll encounter street vendors selling souvenirs, food, or other items. While some are legitimate, others may sell overpriced or low-quality goods. Stick to established shops and avoid engaging with overly aggressive vendors.

Health Considerations

1. **Stay Hydrated**: Rome can get very hot, especially in the summer months. Bring a refillable water bottle, as there are water fountains (nasoni) around the city where you can fill up. Staying hydrated is crucial, particularly if you plan to spend several hours exploring the Colosseum.

2. **Wear Comfortable Shoes**: The Colosseum's terrain includes uneven surfaces, stairs, and

cobblestones. Comfortable, sturdy shoes are essential to prevent slips and falls, and to keep your feet comfortable during extended walking tours.

3. **Be Cautious of Sun Exposure**: If visiting during the day, be prepared for sun exposure, as shade can be limited. Wear sunscreen, a hat, and sunglasses, and take breaks in shaded areas to avoid heat exhaustion.

4. **Know Your Limits**: The Colosseum involves a lot of walking and stair climbing. If you have mobility issues or health concerns, consider opting for a guided tour that can accommodate your needs, or limit your exploration to the more accessible areas.

Emergency Contacts in Rome

Key Emergency Numbers

- **112 – General Emergency Number**: This is the universal emergency number in Italy and throughout the European Union. By dialing 112, you can reach the police, medical services, and fire brigade. Operators speak multiple languages, making it accessible for travelers. This number should be your first point of contact in any emergency.

- **113 – Police**: If you require immediate police assistance, dial 113. This number connects you directly to the local police (Polizia di Stato) who can respond to crimes, accidents, or any situation requiring law enforcement.

- **118 – Medical Emergencies**: For urgent medical assistance, dial 118. This will connect you to the medical emergency services (Servizio Sanitario di Urgenza ed Emergenza) who can dispatch ambulances and provide first aid instructions over the phone.

- **115 – Fire Department**: In case of a fire or similar emergencies, dialing 115 will connect you to the fire department (Vigili del Fuoco). They can also assist in situations such as gas leaks or other hazards.

Accessing Emergency Numbers Quickly

It is recommended that you save these emergency numbers in your phone contacts before your trip. Label them clearly (e.g., "Italy Emergency - 112") so that you can find them quickly if needed. Additionally, most modern smartphones allow you to make emergency calls without unlocking the phone. Familiarize yourself with this feature on your device.

In the event of an emergency where you cannot speak, dialing 112 or 118 and staying on the line can allow operators to trace your location. Always stay calm and provide as much information as possible to ensure help arrives swiftly.

Additional Resources

- **Embassy Contacts**: It is also advisable to have the contact details of your country's embassy in Rome. They can assist with lost passports, legal issues, or serious incidents.

- **Local Hospitals**: Knowing the location of nearby hospitals, especially those with English-speaking staff, can be invaluable. Some of the main hospitals in Rome include Policlinico Umberto I and Ospedale San Giovanni.

- **Pharmacies**: Pharmacies (Farmacia) in Rome can provide minor medical assistance and advice. Many are open 24/7, with the locations of the nearest open pharmacy typically displayed on the doors of all pharmacies.

Health Tips & Nearby Medical Facilities

Staying Healthy During Your Visit

When visiting the Colosseum, it's essential to take steps to stay healthy, ensuring your experience is enjoyable and stress-free. Rome's warm climate, particularly in the summer, can lead to dehydration and heat exhaustion. To avoid these, make sure to drink plenty of water throughout the day. Bring a refillable water bottle, as there are many public fountains (known as "nasoni") around the city where you can fill up for free.

Wear comfortable shoes, as exploring the Colosseum and its surrounding areas involves a lot of walking on uneven surfaces. Applying sunscreen and wearing a hat are also crucial to protect yourself from the sun, especially during peak hours.

If you have specific dietary needs, research nearby restaurants in advance to find options that cater to your requirements. Rome offers a variety of dining choices, including gluten-free and vegetarian-friendly establishments.

Nearby Medical Facilities

In the event that you require medical assistance during your visit to the Colosseum, several medical facilities are conveniently located nearby. The most prominent one is the **Ospedale San Giovanni Addolorata**, located about 2 kilometers from the Colosseum. This hospital is well equipped with emergency services and is easily accessible by taxi or public transport.

For minor medical issues, such as needing a prescription or treating a small injury, local pharmacies ("farmacie") can be very helpful. Pharmacies in Italy are marked with a green cross and are staffed by knowledgeable pharmacists who can provide over-the-counter medications and advice. There is a pharmacy close to the Colosseum, **Farmacia Colosseo**, located on Via di San Giovanni in Laterano.

What to Do in Case of a Medical Emergency

If you experience a medical emergency while at the Colosseum, call the emergency number **112**, which is the general emergency number for police, fire, and medical services in Italy. Operators speak multiple languages and will dispatch the necessary help immediately.

For less urgent situations, consider visiting a local pharmacy or walk-in medical center. If you need to see a doctor but it is not an emergency, you can also ask your hotel for assistance, as many hotels have partnerships with local medical services and can arrange for a doctor to visit you directly.

Common Scams to Avoid

1. The Fake Tour Guide Scam

Scammers posing as official tour guides may approach you near the Colosseum, offering "discounted" or "exclusive" tours. These individuals often have no official credentials and may provide little to no valuable information. To avoid this, always book tours through reputable agencies or directly at the official Colosseum ticket office. Look for guides wearing official badges and avoid anyone who seems overly pushy.

2. Ticket Scalping

Beware of individuals selling Colosseum tickets on the street, often at inflated prices or for non-existent tours. These tickets might be fake or invalid, leaving you unable to enter. Purchase your tickets only from the official Colosseum website, licensed tour companies, or at the authorized ticket counters. If a scalper approaches you, politely decline and walk away.

3. The Bracelet Scam

This fraud is common not just near the Colosseum but throughout Rome. Friendly individuals, often posing as street vendors, may try to tie a "free" bracelet or string around your wrist. Once it is on, they will demand payment, sometimes aggressively. To avoid this, firmly say no and keep your hands to yourself. If someone tries to grab your wrist, step back and move away quickly.

4. The Photo Opportunity Scam

Street performers dressed as gladiators or Roman soldiers near the Colosseum often invite tourists to take photos with them. After the photo is taken, they may demand an exorbitant fee. To avoid this, always ask about the cost before taking any photos. If the fee seems unreasonable, politely decline the offer.

5. Pickpocketing

The areas around the Colosseum, especially during peak hours, are hotspots for pickpockets. These thieves work in groups and may use distractions such as bumping into you or dropping something to divert your attention. Keep your valuables secure in a money belt or an inside pocket. Be particularly vigilant in crowded areas, and never leave your bags unattended.

6. Fake Charity Donations

Scammers might approach you with a clipboard, asking for donations for a charity. These "charities" are often bogus, and any money you give goes directly into the scammer's pocket. Politely decline any such requests, and if you wish to donate, do so through verified organizations.

CONCLUSION

As we draw the curtains on this comprehensive guide to the Colosseum, it is clear that this ancient marvel is more than just a structure of stone and history—it is a living testament to the grandeur of Rome and the spirit of its people. Through these pages, we have journeyed together from the foundational stones of this iconic amphitheater to the vibrant culture and timeless traditions that continue to pulse through the heart of the Eternal City.

We began by exploring the rich historical tapestry that the Colosseum weaves into the story of Rome. We delved into the architectural genius that constructed this monumental arena and the cultural significance that made it the epicenter of public life in ancient times. The tales of gladiators, emperors, and the roaring crowds have brought to life an era of spectacle and power, reminding us of the Colosseum's enduring place in the world.

As we have navigated the practical aspects of visiting— from planning your trip to exploring the intricate corridors of the Colosseum itself—we have ensured that you are well prepared for an unforgettable experience. We have highlighted the special tours and events that offer a unique perspective, shared tips for capturing the perfect photograph, and pointed you towards the lesser known in the surrounding area. Whether you are marveling at the ancient ruins of the Roman Forum or enjoying a quiet moment with a gelato at a nearby café, the Colosseum serves as a constant reminder of Rome's rich heritage and its ability to inspire awe.

Moreover, we have taken care to prepare you for the journey with essential cultural tips, safety advice, and recommendations for accommodations and dining. The surrounding neighborhoods, filled with both luxury and budget-friendly options, offer a glimpse into daily Roman life, while the culinary delights of traditional Roman cuisine await your discovery.

However, the Colosseum is not just about the past; it is a bridge to the present and a gateway to countless other adventures. The nearby attractions, from the tranquil gardens of Tivoli to the historical depths of Ostia Antica, promise to enrich your journey, making every moment in Rome a chapter in your own story.

As you stand at the threshold of history, ready to embark on your journey to the Colosseum, remember that this is more than just a visit—it is a pilgrimage to the cradle of Western civilization. The stones beneath your feet have witnessed the rise and fall of empires, and now, they invite you to walk among the echoes of the past.

Rome, with its timeless beauty and vibrant culture, is waiting to welcome you. The Colosseum, in all its ancient grandeur, stands ready to share its stories with you. So pack your bags, book your tickets, and prepare to step into history.

Whether you are a history buff, an architecture enthusiast, or simply a traveler seeking new experiences, the Colosseum promises a journey unlike any other. Let this be your call to action—do not just read about the Colosseum, come and live it. Stand in its shadows, feel the history, and let Rome's eternal flame ignite your passion for discovery.

Your adventure awaits. The Colosseum is calling. Will you answer?

APPENDICES

Useful Phrases in Italian

Greetings and Polite Expressions

- **Buongiorno** (bwohn-johr-noh) - Good morning / Good day
- **Buonasera** (bwohn-ah-seh-rah) - Good evening
- **Ciao** (chow) - Hello / Goodbye (informal)
- **Arrivederci** (ahr-ree-veh-dehr-chee) - Goodbye (formal)
- **Per favore** (pehr fah-voh-reh) - Please
- **Grazie** (grah-tsyeh) - Thank you
- **Prego** (preh-goh) - You are welcome
- **Mi scusi** (mee skooh-zee) - Excuse me (formal) / I'm sorry

Asking for Help and Directions

- **Dov'è il Colosseo?** (doh-veh eel koh-loh-seh-oh) - Where is the Colosseum?
- **Può aiutarmi?** (pwoh ah-you-tahr-mee) - Can you help me?
- **Come si arriva a…?** (koh-meh see ah-ree-vah ah) - How do you get to…?

158

- **A che ora apre?** (ah keh oh-rah ah-preh) - What time does it open?
- **A che ora chiude?** (ah keh oh-rah kyoo-deh) - What time does it close?

Ordering Food and Drinks

- **Vorrei…** (voh-rreh) - I would like…
- **Un caffè, per favore** (oon kah-feh, pehr fah-voh-reh) - A coffee, please
- **Il conto, per favore** (eel kohn-toh, pehr fah-voh-reh) - The bill, please
- **È delizioso!** (eh deh-lee-tsee-oh-zoh) - It's delicious!
- **Acqua naturale / frizzante** (ahk-kwah nah-too-rah-leh / freet-tsahn-teh) - Still / sparkling water

Basic Questions and Responses

- **Quanto costa?** (kwahn-toh koh-stah) - How much does it cost?
- **Dove sono i bagni?** (doh-veh soh-noh ee bahn-yee) - Where are the restrooms?
- **Sì / No** (see / noh) - Yes / No
- **Parla inglese?** (par-lah een-gleh-zeh) - Do you speak English?

- **Non capisco** (nohn kah-pees-koh) - I don't understand

- **Può ripetere, per favore?** (pwoh ree-peh-teh-reh, pehr fah-voh-reh) - Can you repeat that, please?

Emergency Phrases

- **Ho bisogno di un dottore** (oh bee-zoh-nyoh dee oon doht-toh-reh) - I need a doctor

- **Chiamate un'ambulanza!** (kee-ah-mah-teh oon-ahm-boo-lahn-tsah) - Call an ambulance!

- **Dov'è l'ospedale più vicino?** (doh-veh loh-speh-dah-leh pyoo vee-chee-noh) - Can you direct me to the closest hospital?

Contacts for Tour Operators and Guides

Walks of Italy

Walks of Italy is a highly respected tour operator offering small group and private tours of the Colosseum. Their guides are experts in Roman history, and their tours often include exclusive access to areas like the underground chambers. You can book their tours online through their website, which provides detailed descriptions of each tour, available dates, and pricing. It is advisable to book in advance, particularly during high tourist seasons.

Contact: +39 06 9480 7475

The Roman Guy

The Roman Guy is known for its well-rounded tours that combine the Colosseum with other key Roman attractions like the Roman Forum and Palatine Hill. They offer a range of tours, including early morning and night tours, which allow you to avoid the crowds. Bookings can be made directly on their website, where you can also find customer reviews and additional tour details.

Contact: +39 06 9480 8378

City Wonders

City Wonders is a popular choice for guided tours of the Colosseum, particularly for first-time visitors. They offer a variety of tour options, including skip-the-line access, which is a huge time-saver. Their website allows for easy online booking, and they offer customer support in multiple languages to assist with any inquiries.

Contact: +39 06 8336 0561

LivItaly Tours

LivItaly Tours specializes in small group tours that provide an intimate and personalized experience. Their Colosseum tours often include special access to restricted areas and are led by expert local guides. Reservations can be made online, and they offer flexible cancellation policies, which is a bonus for travelers with uncertain schedules.

Contact: +39 06 8895 6646

Context Travel

Context Travel offers in-depth, scholarly tours led by historians and archaeologists. Their tours are perfect for travelers who want a deeper understanding of the Colosseum's history and architecture. You can book their tours online, where you can choose from various themes and levels of detail.

Contact: +39 06 4522 1818

How to Book in Advance

Booking your Colosseum tour in advance is highly recommended, especially during peak travel seasons. Most tour operators offer online booking through their websites, where you can select your preferred date, time, and type of tour. It is advisable to book at least a few weeks in advance to secure your spot, particularly for tours that offer special access or are limited to small groups. Additionally, many operators offer flexible cancellation policies, allowing you to adjust your plans if needed.

Printed in Dunstable, United Kingdom

67770782R00097